GWEN ROCKWOOD

Reporting Live

from the
Laundry
Pile

THE ROCKWOOD FILES COLLECTION

THREE PEAKS PRESS

Cover and chapter photos by Lisa Mac Photography
Lisa's photos also appear on pages 35, 61, 67, 114, 120, 149 & 160

Designed by Moody Image
Text set in Garamond

ISBN-13: 978-0615659800

For Mom, Dad, Greg and Tom, with love

Acknowledgements:

Thank you, thank you, thank you….

…to my mom and dad, Wanda and Billy Rule, whose love and encouragement have made all the difference. And to my late brother, Greg, who nudges me along from above.

…to my husband Tom, who pushed me to tackle this dream and make it real.

…to my kids Adam, Jack and Kate, who always let me take mental notes when they do something funny. Thanks, kids, for leaving me alone long enough at the computer to finish the book. The three of you are my very best, most important work, and I love you.

…to my friend and editor, Ritta Martin Basu, who can tell it like it is and still be kind and inspiring at the same time. Your guidance has been invaluable.

…to my friend and business partner, Shannon Magsam, who bubbles over with personality and brilliant ideas (including the title of this book) and whose idea to launch a website (nwaMotherlode.com) put us in business together four years ago. I'm thankful for our "God thing."

…to Greg Moody of Moody Image, whose design talent has made me love the look of this book. Knowing you were just an e-mail away made this process so much better.

…to Lisa McSpadden, whose photographs hit me where I live. Your work has brought the book to a whole new level, and I thank you for your vision.

…to the editors of my weekly newspaper column, The Rockwood Files, who have graciously allowed me space in their newspapers to tell these stories.

…to the readers of my newspaper column whose notes, comments and emails over the years have been my "gold." I thank you so much for your kindness.

…to my friends, especially the "Stuttgart Girls" Jennifer, Alaina and Christy, who have been my buddies since grade school. Your friendship is a treasure.

…to John Cash, for reading the Sunday comics to me as a kid and for making me want to grow up to be as funny and wonderful as you are.

…to the late Donna Johnson Herring, whose handwritten letters and cards over the years encouraged me to keep writing.

…to my teachers, including Nancy Butler, Phyllis Orlicek and James Gamble, who wrote notes in the margins of my school essays that made me believe maybe I really could be a writer one day.

And to Our Heavenly Father, who breathes creativity into all of us.

Table of Contents

Reporting Live from the Laundry Pile:
The Rockwood Files Collection

Each week I sit down to face the blank page. After hours of wrestling words and playing with phrases, I hit the send button and another 700-word chunk of my life wings its way through cyberspace to the inboxes of a dozen newspaper editors who print my weekly column, The Rockwood Files. I turned in my first column when I was 22 years old while working as an assistant in a newsroom, and I've done it every Tuesday since for the past 17 years.

If I let myself think about it too much, being a columnist strikes me as one of the most obnoxiously self-important careers a person could have. Who am I to assume people want to read about my life? I'm not scaling Mount Everest with no legs, and I don't have a million Twitter followers.

What I write about is the funny thing that happened on the way to somewhere. I write about that childhood fishing trip and the day my parents met. I write about the ways my husband drives me nuts when he won't just admit he's not a freaking plumber.

I write love letters to cheesecake and rants about ugly recliners. I write about the dogs and the cat and our three kids and kindergarten shots, jump shots, sleepwalking, Silly Putty, full frontal nudity, Barbies, a chipmunk spotting, Halloween pranks and a terrifying run-in with a 20-foot snake. It's all here and more.

But it's just everyday life. Is it worthy of a spot in the newspaper where reports about political maneuvering, business deals and important, life-and-death events are recorded?

Yeah, it is. And it's taken nearly two decades for me to stop feeling apologetic about it. I know now, after years of letters and emails from readers, that people need stories about everyday life. They give us valuable moments of connection with each other – moments that hold us together in what can often feel like a fragmented world.

I wish I could say I write the column solely for that noble reason -- to give the sense of connection, a moment of "Oh, me too!" or "I know exactly what you mean." But the truth is I write because I need to. For as long as I remember, the page has been my secret fort under the stairs. It's the friend I crack jokes to, and it's my therapist's couch. It's the way I hear myself think and make sense of things. And it's how I make peace with things that'll never make sense.

When my older brother died suddenly in 2001, I didn't write anything for weeks. The day I finally picked up a notebook again, I poured my grief onto the page because I felt like it would swallow me whole if I didn't.

And then something remarkable happened. Those newspaper readers – the same ones who'd chuckled about the everyday funny things I'd written – they felt the pain with me. And for weeks I was blessed with compassionate notes and emails from people who understood -- people who'd endured a "terrible news" phone call of their own, people with their own pain.

The experience helped me realize that, as long as I'm honest with the page and the people who read it, my simple newspaper column about everyday life can be just as valid as the hard news surrounding it. As it turns out, everyday life is the important stuff.

The columns collected here represent a few of the stories I've written during these 17 years. I've sorted them into themes the same way I sort laundry when it overflows its basket. As I compiled the columns, I laughed at some of the stories I'd forgotten, and other times I cringed at the voice of the younger me. Reading stories you wrote a decade ago is a little like looking at photos from junior high school – the frosted blue eye shadow and bad perm years.

But even the embarrassing stuff offers a snapshot of the journey that led to where I stand today -- smack in the middle of an everyday life. To the readers who have read me as I've "grown up" and to those who may have just stumbled on the book -- I thank you for spending part of your everyday life with me. My connection to you is the best fringe benefit a writer could ever hope for.

CHAPTER 1

THE MARRIAGE FILE

The "Up" Side of Stood Up

Sometimes the greatest love stories begin when someone gets dumped. In the summer of 1961, a 17-year-old country girl was stood up for a date to the Camp Doughboy annual carnival and dance. Her older brother convinced her to tag along with him and his date.

She was standing uncomfortably against the wall, watching couples whirl across the floor, when a boy approached and asked for a dance. She'd seen him before. He was hard to miss. He had danced with just about every girl in the place, and when he ran out of girls he grabbed a stuffed teddy bear he won at the fair and twirled it around like it was the princess at the ball.

She agreed to the dance and spent almost the entire evening in place of the bear, waltzing, jitterbugging and twisting. At the end of the night, he offered to drive her home but she refused. Smart girls don't just jump into anybody's car, no matter how well he dances.

She went home with her brother, cautiously agreeing to let the boy pick her up at home for the next night's dance. Then she convinced two friends to double date with her and the new guy the next night. They piled into his gray 1955 Ford Custom and headed for the dance.

Perhaps it was that second night when their dance steps began to lead into a future. But he swears to this day it was her grandmother's fresh lemonade that kept him coming back to the country to see her. After a year of lemonade, everyone knew it was much more than that.

After she graduated from high school and got her first job, the couple eloped to Memphis because neither family had enough money for a formal wedding. There was no fancy dress or floral arrangements, no slick ice sculptures, no tiered cake, and only inexpensive gold wedding bands.

As for wedding photos, there are two black-and-white snapshots: One of her standing by the car outside the chapel and one of him

3

standing by the car outside the chapel. There are no pictures of them together because they were the only ones on the trip.

Fifty years later, those snapshots of my mother and father are still two of my favorites in the family photo album. Out of such a simple, sparse beginning grew one of the longest and best love stories I've seen.

It might be sweet if I could tell you the reason this simple beginning has led to 50 years of marriage is because they both continually shower each other with romantic gestures, gifts and cards. But the truth is simpler than that.

Their strength comes from a sense of practical partnership. Partners in loving two children, partners in paying bills, partners in struggling through hard times and laughing through good ones. They've never read books about how to keep the romance alive and they don't go to marriage seminars.

Their romance is just between the two of them, but I see glimpses of it when they're back on the dance floor at a friend's fancy wedding reception. I see evidence of it in their standing Friday night dates for a catfish dinner on the town.

They don't expect an orchestra to start playing every time they come home, and they never see an argument as the end of the world. Neither one of them expects perfection or continual romance. Only continued partnership, continued support.

I did catch them holding hands recently as we made our way to a college football game. I asked if they were getting sweet and lovey-dovey in their old age. My dad's quick come-back was, "No. We're just holding each other up."

Perhaps the strongest love is not the kind that greeting cards are written about. Maybe love is best when romance is the icing, when the main goal is to keep "holding each other up."

IN THE BEGINNING

This love story begins with a blind date and low expectations. After all, I'd been on blind dates before and come away with nothing but the strong desire to never be fixed up again. But Lillian talked me into it. She said he was taller than me, cute and employed – a solid start. And she and another mutual friend, Gary, agreed to come along and serve as my blind date air bag, in case it crashed and burned.

So there we sat in the restaurant – me and the two mutual friends.

Waiting.

Waiting.

Waiting for my blind date to show up.

At the "ten minutes late" mark, Lillian and Gary fidgeted nervously at the unspoken possibility that perhaps I was being stood up. I, on the other hand, wasn't nervous at all. The blind dates I'd had in the past had trained the high expectations right out of me. Worst case scenario, if the guy didn't show, I'd still get a free meal because Lil and Gary would feel terrible about it. So I was covered either way. It sounds jaded, but dating can do that to a girl.

Finally, my date Tom rushed in with explanations about a meeting that ran long – blah, blah, blah. Our friends introduced us, and he was cuter than I expected. Then he asked how long I'd been working as a newspaper editor – only he got the name of the newspaper wrong and instead mentioned my company's competitor. So five minutes into the blind date, he'd racked up two strikes: he arrived late, and he couldn't get the details straight.

The rest of dinner was pleasant enough, but he mostly talked business with Gary, who was also one of his clients. And I talked mainly to Lil who'd gotten us all into this thing in the first place.

Dinner ended and, in the absence of any real sparks, the blind date was ending with it. But Gary had these college basketball tickets and the game was just about to start. "Why don't we all go to the game?" he said. So we went, partly because we couldn't think of a reason not to and partly because our friends were trying so hard to give us a nudge.

We found a parking spot on campus on a steep, rain-slick hill. I hesitated as we began to walk down it because, having come straight from the office, I was still wearing a pantsuit and high heels with no traction. The last thing I needed was to slip and end up sprawled spread-eagle on the pavement in front of this guy I hardly knew.

And that's when it happened. A short little exchange that turned the whole course of events. Seeing my hesitation, Tom held out his arm and said "Do you want to hang on to me?" And I said, "Yes, because if I go down then I'm taking you with me." And he laughed, not a fake, blind date kind of laugh but a real one.

Then I laughed, not a "God I wish this was over" kind of laugh but the real thing. And somehow, in that brief moment, the evening shifted into a different gear. During the game we talked, joked, even flirted a little. That date led to a second, a third and, almost two years later, to marriage vows.

Our blind date was nearly 16 years ago. I can still pinpoint the beginning of our relationship to that exact moment at the top of the steep hill when we laughed and locked arms to walk down together. Laughter gave us the start. And, for us and lots of other couples, it's the glue that keeps us going.

Love and passion are great. Everybody wants love and passion. But so much of day-to-day life is like that steep, rain-slick hill – hard to navigate, scary, sometimes treacherous. And if you don't walk it with someone who can help you laugh, even through your missteps, you're toast. You'll never make it.

Over two years of dating and almost 14 years of marriage, Tom and I have been through job changes, house moves, miscarriages, the death of my only sibling, and three new babies who have taught us what life is about. I'm grateful for the love and passion, the commitment, the loyalty and friendship. But more than anything, I'm thankful for the laughter – the everyday, get-you-through-anything laughter. And I hope that 50 years from now, we'll still be laughing.

The First Garage Sale

A marriage is the coming together of two lives, two hearts and two minds – that's the easy part. What people don't tell you is that marriage is also the coming together of two sets of household stuff, and that's where things get tricky.

Take Person A, who's been trekking along through life, collecting his own stuff for many years. Now add him to Person B, who also has her own perfectly good stuff. What you end up with is a lot of duplicate, uncoordinated, mismatched stuff and the overwhelming need for a garage sale.

So that's exactly what my new husband Tom and I decided to do. And for about five minutes, we were as cute and nauseating as we could be about it. "Ah, our first garage sale together," we cooed. We'd get up early. We'd buy doughnuts. We'd sit in lawn chairs and collect our money in a shoebox. It'd be great.

I ran the ad in the newspaper. Tom bought the signs pointing people to our driveway. All that was left to do was collect our stuff, price it and slap it on a card table. Sounded easy enough.

But deciding whose stuff would meet its fate in the garage sale was far from easy. It was obvious to me that his things were most deserving of a spot on the driveway. Surely he knew that the hulking green fake plant in the corner was horrible. I thought he understood that we didn't need stereo speakers bigger than most foreign cars. And I always assumed he was eager to unload that horrible floor lamp with the cheap glass table tutu around its mid-section. But, much to my surprise, he thought this was his good stuff.

I was even more shocked to learn that he had almost no appreciation for the majority of my good stuff. He wanted to sell my futon two-seater sofa. I explained how this was the first piece of furniture I'd ever bought on my own and that I'd studied for final exams on this very sofa for four years straight and that I actually owed my college education to the comfort of this benevolent couch.

He said it was "ugly." Obviously, one person's "ugly" is another person's "character."

After a few rounds, we finally came up with a mutually acceptable pile of stuff to be sold come sun-up, but that was only half the battle. Pricing is where things really get hairy. When you're a newlywed, you want to protect your spouse's feelings. You don't want to tell him his combined garage sale assets have an approximate net worth of 75 cents. So we each priced our own things, went to bed and waited for daybreak and the first customer.

We didn't have to wait long. We soon discovered that serious garage sale shoppers don't wait for daybreak. They circle their prey in the wee hours of the morning, waiting for the sun and the garage door to come up. Then they spring from their cars, scramble up the drive and descend like locusts. These are not your average shoppers. They're the Green Berets of garage sales, picking off a bargain from blocks away. And they're the Navy Seals of negotiating.

9

We held strong during the first hour. There was no way we could accept $2 for a perfectly good electric can opener. No way. But as the morning wore on and the doughnuts ran out, we started to weaken.

"How much for your husband's neckties?" one man asked me.

"I'll take one dollar for the entire box of them if you can get 'em out of here before he gets back from the bathroom," I said.

Sold.

But then, when my back was turned, Tom sold my bookcase for $5. A large, perfectly good piece of furniture and he let it go for less than we pay to eat at Arby's. I was astonished. He said it was revenge for the mammoth stereo speakers I "accidentally" sold for $30 for the pair when he really wanted $30 each.

We went on this way until almost noon, when we realized that everything we didn't sell would have to be re-boxed and brought back into the house. So in the final hour, we slashed prices, agreeing to throw in the card table if someone would just take the stuff away.

At noon, we gathered the remaining scraps of our sale and drove it to a charity drop-off. We used some of our proceeds to pay for lunch and then returned home to take a nap. We had survived our first garage sale. We felt we'd passed one of the first milestones of our marriage.

Now, all we have to do is agree on how to redecorate the house. Sounds easy enough...

A Housework Hottie

After a couple years of marriage, you begin to understand that there's only one thing as attractive as a man in a tuxedo – a man holding a can of Pledge and a dust rag.

I realized this profound truth last weekend when I was sick. I told Tom I should really get out of bed since I had housework to do, but I was so tired and congested. Hours later, I woke from a nap to the strong scent of aerosol lemons in the air. I wandered into the living room and there he was – stooped over the coffee table wiping it down the same way he waxes the hood of the car. I was shocked. I had no idea he even knew what Pledge was, much less what cabinet I kept it in.

Surely the stars must have been in alignment that day because he went on to clean the entire house. Dusting, dishes, laundry, vacuuming, bathrooms and yes – even mopping. I watched amazed from my sickbed, and it was then that I realized just how good a man looks when he's pushing a vacuum cleaner across the bedroom. It was heavenly. He was like a domesticated George Clooney with the power to disinfect.

It's times like these when a woman realizes just how much has changed since her single days. Back then, my idea of sexy was a Chippendale body in a fireman's uniform. But now, nothing looks better than the sight of my husband, in his old T-shirt and jeans, standing in our shower with a can of Scrubbing Bubbles.

Of course, I'm not the only married woman affected by the sight of a man doing housework. My dad has always known that the way to my mother's heart was through a clean kitchen. His dishwashing and countertop scrubbing have served him well over the years, as a kind of "Get Out of the Dog House Free" card. His dishpan hands have worked more magic than any bouquet of flowers ever could. In fact, my mother now has a picture hanging in her kitchen that reads "No Man Was Ever Shot By His Wife While Doing the Dishes."

If only more men understood the power of housework, the divorce rate would surely plummet. How can you argue with a man who's willing to not only take out the trash but also clean out the refrigerator? It's impossible.

Men, there really is an easy way to make your wife's heart race with desire. Just spend less time pumping iron and more time pushing a mop. Less time worrying about losing your hair and more time cleaning it out of the drain in the shower. You get the idea.

And if you can do all this without being asked, then your "good husband" points are automatically tripled. And if you do it just to keep your sick wife from getting out of bed, your rating goes off the charts. She'll be bragging to her friends for weeks.

If you really want to sweep a woman off her feet, start by sweeping her kitchen floor. Not everyone can be George Clooney. But any man can become a "housework hottie."

THROWING MONEY DOWN A HOLE

Tom is a saver. Not cheap, mind you. But definitely a saver. I, on the other hand, have always been the "Life is short and why have money if you can't enjoy it" type of girl. Like most couples, we've had a few disagreements over money. But seven years of marriage have helped both of us meet in the middle. He no longer pinches every penny. And I, who used to never flinch at paying full price, have learned to appreciate the thrill of getting a good deal, which brings me to this story.

When we moved into our house eight months ago, it was surrounded by beautiful trees overlooking a barren yard. The grass was almost completely dead and all that remained was a brown dustbowl dotted with dying sprigs. So this year our spring project was growing a lawn. But first we needed to repair the sprinkler system and install a separate water meter.

Our plumber came by and gave a cost estimate. He explained that the actual plumbing wouldn't take much time, but digging the hole would. Then he added, "If you want to save some money, you could dig the hole yourselves."

Tom's eyes lit up when he heard those three little words: "save some money." We agreed to dig a rather wide hole down to the pipes so the plumber could return in a few days and get right to work. To be fair, I knew that "we" wouldn't be digging the hole. It would be the "he" part of "we" who would have to do it. My philosophy is that the person who gives birth to the babies should be excused from all future manual labor, particularly dirty excavation projects.

Last Saturday, Tom set out with his shovel and our two sons to teach the manly art of hole-digging. More than an hour passed, and the boys were getting tired of throwing dirt clods at each other. I went outside to check the progress. "This ground is as hard as rock and there are tree roots everywhere!" Tom said. "How far down are these pipes anyway?" I sensed that the money-saving mission wasn't going well.

"Do you want me to have the plumber finish this for us?" I asked, which was wife-code for "Please, oh please let the plumber finish this before you throw your back out again." But Tom insisted on pressing forward and disappeared into the garage to get heavier digging artillery. When he came back with a large pickaxe, I gathered the kids and headed for the safety of the kitchen.

Half an hour later, the boys were enjoying grilled cheese sandwiches at the kitchen table while I washed dishes. Suddenly, the full stream of water coming from the faucet dwindled to a trickle and then stopped. Minutes later, Tom burst through the door wearing wet clothes and a look of complete frustration. The hole was dug, but the pickaxe had found the pipe first and sliced right through it, creating a large geyser in the front yard.

Tom turned the water off to our house so the geyser would stop gushing and attracting stares from neighbors. Then we tried to decide what to do next. We could call the plumber but then we'd have to pay the Saturday after-hours rate. Or we could pack up the boys and go to a local hotel so we'd have access to running water and wait for Monday morning. Either way, we'd end up spending more money than the hole-digging project was supposed to save. The cruel irony of it all was torture for Tom. But we knew it was time to call in the professional. Within 20 minutes, the plumber had fixed the pipe. Because he's a nice guy who has been fixing our plumbing for years now, he gave us a "frequent flyer" rate so the mishap didn't cost much. Tom was satisfied that the effort had been worth it because, technically, we'd still saved a little money.

Later that evening, Tom's lower back muscles began to rebel against swinging that pickaxe. As he did a painful impersonation of the hunchback of Notre Dame, we realized the small amount of money we saved would likely go toward paying the doctor's not-so-small bill. In the end, we gave new meaning to the phrase "throwing money down a hole."

Style Wars

There's a reason why there are so many old sofas and chairs in American homes. It's not because consumers don't like change, and it's not because furniture is so expensive. It's because a husband and wife only agree on the same sofa or chair about once every other decade.

Tom and I will celebrate our 10th wedding anniversary in November, and we're blessed because we agree on lots of things like parenting, religion, politics and even what shows to watch on TV. But every time we walk into a furniture store and I see him sidle up to the ugliest chair in the joint, I wonder "Who is this man, and why is he trying to make me crazy?"

If you asked him, Tom would say I started this style war years ago when we married and merged furniture. We were about to move to a new city, and there was one piece of Tom's furniture I thought should be left off the moving truck. It was a leather burgundy recliner. And I'm being kind when I say it was "style challenged" – puffy and tufted in all the wrong places.

I convinced Tom that it had to go because it wouldn't look right with our other furniture. He reluctantly agreed, and I sold that burgundy beast faster than you can say "classified ad." But he has never let me forget it, and often he reminisces about just how much he loved that chair, how comfortable it was, how much he misses it – as if I'd ripped him away from a faux-leather Siamese twin.

I did replace the burgundy beast with a more suitable wingback recliner chair that he liked just fine and took many naps in. But last year two of the chair's springs snapped off and the frame got wobbly. We had it repaired once, but lately it's making creaks and squeaks even when the kids crawl into it. So we're back in the market for a new chair.

This time I've got a decade of marriage under my belt and I've learned a thing or two about what men want. And one thing they want is a chair of their own where they can stretch out and relax, watch TV and doze off after they've eaten too much pot roast. Typically, these men will not argue about the other furnishings in the house, mostly because they just don't care. But when it comes to THE chair – they care, a lot.

So this time I resolved to let Tom pick out the recliner so he'd be sure to have something he truly loved. We walked into a furniture store today, and right away I saw several chairs that might be perfect. They're recliners that don't look like recliners – a rare, new breed of chair designed to give men comfort while giving women style at the same time. Tom checked them out and picked one he said was especially comfortable. But just to be sure, he wanted to walk the store to see if anything else caught his eye.

Then, it did.

As if drawn by some kind of bizarre man magnet, his eyes locked on a recliner at the back of the store. It was a big, puffy rocker that looked like a beefier first cousin to the burgundy beast I'd sold so long ago. When Tom sank down into it, his eyes lit up and he said, "Oh, yeah…"

The male salesperson pointed out that this particular recliner comes with an attached remote control massager, probably because this guy knows that the only thing a man loves more than an ugly recliner is an ugly recliner with bells and whistles.

The chair reminded me of the Michelin Man, with rolls upon rolls of bloated foam padding covered with wrinkly leather. But I didn't say anything because I'd promised to be open-minded. Tom said, "Sit down and try it out, honey." So I did, and I'll admit the chair feels fabulous – like a vibrating bed of Twinkies. It'd be great if I could just wear a blindfold every time I walked into the room.

He narrowed it down to two choices today – a nice-looking chair you'd never guess was a recliner and the massive, puffy chair with massager. At this point, it could go either way. Maybe I'll get lucky.

If I don't and he picks the Michelin Man chair with built-in massager, I'll just have to bite my lip real hard and remember I made vows to this man – to love him for better or for worse, even when "worse" comes to live in our living room.

"Out, Out Damn Spot"

Most men don't fully understand this, but sometimes a woman walks into a room in her house and knows, with certainty, that something has GOT to change. It happened to me when I walked into the guest room and realized I was sick of the varying degrees of beige in there. It felt dull, lifeless.

So I chose a color, and Tom painted the room a cool, airy blue that I love. But repainting triggered a chain of redecorating events. The old bedspread didn't go with the new blue, so I switched it out with one that does. Then the peeling finish on the nightstands screamed for attention.

I started repainting the nightstands after Tom left for a business trip. My parents had come for a visit that weekend, and I recruited my dad for a little father-daughter painting project. We spread out a paint tarp in the garage and began the long sanding process. Once the hard part was done, we used spray paint to speed up the job.

Nearly drunk on paint fumes, I suggested we move the nightstands onto the driveway to do the second coat of paint in the open air. It wasn't until I started spraying the nightstand's legs that I realized we hadn't moved the tarp.

"Uh oh," I said. "I just painted the driveway."

"Oh well," Dad said. "It'll wear off."

I agreed and went right on spraying until the nightstands were a beautiful glossy white. I couldn't wait to show the paint job to Tom when he came home. About 10 seconds after he returned home and hugged me and the kids, he asked, "Why are there white spots on the driveway?"

"I repainted those old nightstands. Want to see them?" I asked.

"And you painted on the driveway without the tarp?" he asked, completely ignoring the bigger fact that I'd painted two nightstands.

"Well, yeah, but it's just the driveway, so it'll wear off in time," I said.

"You've gotta get those spots off. It's going to drive me crazy," he said.

I agreed to the spot removal just to appease him and then promptly filed it away at the bottom of my "to do" list, knowing the likelihood of me getting around to doing it was somewhere between "remote chance" and "never gonna happen."

Fast forward one week, and the subject of spots suddenly resurfaced again:

"You know, I asked you a week ago to clean those paint spots off the driveway, and you still haven't done it," he said, perturbed.

"Tom, it's the DRIVEWAY. Why does this bother you so much?" I asked, wondering if the spots had, indeed, driven him crazy.

"They just do! And don't act like you don't have weird things that drive you crazy because you do," he fired back.

I scanned my list of personal quirks, trying to think of something as seemingly trivial as the spots-on-the-driveway issue. Couldn't come up with a single one.

"Okay, so what do I get all worked up about that seems ridiculous to you?" I asked, certain he wouldn't be able to think of anything.

"One word," he said. "Countertops."

Silence.

He had me there, and I knew it. I do come a little unhinged when he leaves things out on the counter and then walks out of the room without putting them away. For me, clean counter space equals a clean mind. Clutter makes me edgy. But I felt certain I could defend my position, so I foolishly pressed forward.

"But you have an English muffin every morning and then leave the kitchen even though your butter knife, jelly jar and crumbs are still RIGHT THERE on the counter!" I said.

"Did it ever occur to you that I might want ANOTHER English muffin so I'm leaving that stuff out on purpose?" he said. "I can't even set a drink down on the counter without you whisking it into the refrigerator when I turn my back."

"Well, that's just crazy," I said, a little flustered and painfully aware that he'd proven his point.

The discussion ended soon after because neither of us could deny our own sore spots. And, ironically enough, his sore spot is an actual spot – on the driveway.

So today, because I took a vow years ago to love and cherish his sanity, I will attempt to remove white paint spots from the driveway. But, if I come inside after restoring the purity of his precious pavement and find a jelly-smeared butter knife on my kitchen counter, I may just have to use it on him.

CHAPTER 2

THE FIRSTBORN FILE

A High-Powered Career

If you'd asked me in my early twenties to make a list of things I'd never do, one of the things on that list would have read "stay home and raise kids." I was all set to be a high-powered career woman. During the years after college graduation, I worked as a newspaper columnist, a reporter, then an editor, then an advertising executive, and then a marketing and public relations director. Things were right on track.

Then a pregnancy test stick showed me the tell-tale second line proving there was a second person involved. Suddenly either I started to change my mind about things or life started to change it for me. Maybe both. I loved my job. It was challenging, rewarding and my co-workers were great. Lots of people would have given almost anything for a position like mine. How could I give it up?

But as the baby in my belly started to grow, so did the mixed emotions about what to do. I was lucky because I could choose. We had enough money for me to stay home with the baby without eating Ramen noodles every night. Some women don't have that option.

I had some friends who knew, without reservation, that they'd be miserable if they left their jobs. But I was sitting squarely on the fence.

One minute, I was sure I'd go back to the office after the baby was born. The next minute, I was certain I couldn't bear to leave him in another woman's arms while I drove off to work.

When I considered leaving my job, I felt apologetic – as if I'd have to turn in my Modern Woman membership card if I didn't forge ahead and become one of the millions of American women proving you can have it all. Could I trade in my business card for a diaper bag and still "count" in a society where profession means so much?

In the end, the decision was hard and easy at the same time. Packing up my office was tough, but once I peered into the face of the new little "boss," the decision seemed easy. More importantly, it felt right.

It's been about a year since that decision. Business lunches with co-workers have been replaced with watching a one-year-old drop Cheerios off the tray of his high chair. A supervisor won't stick his head in my office to say, "Hey, great job on that poopy diaper you just cleaned up." The work is more solitary, but the perks of being here for moments big and small are pretty incredible.

The year at home has taught me I can still be a high-powered career woman, minus the boardroom and the long hours. My career has become raising a good human being, which is as powerful as it gets – one where the stakes are higher than anything. And despite what some would say, I never feel like I've "wasted my education" by jumping off the corporate ladder. Good parents are, above all else, teachers.

Like any job, there are days when I feel like I've made major progress and other days that are a blur of spit-up, dirty dishes and really bad Barney songs. But after a year as a stay-at-home parent, I can say the same things about this job as I did about the last one: I love my job. It's challenging, rewarding and the people are great. Lots of women would give almost anything to have a position like mine.

Why would I ever give all this up?

I Am Man, Hear Me Roar

In this evolved age of parenting, we like to believe we don't influence our kids with the same old gender stereotypes. After all, there are plenty of little boys who pretend to cook using pink, plastic kitchen sets. And I've yet to meet a little girl who doesn't enjoy swinging a toy hammer at chunky plastic nails. But at some point, as their language skills develop, we want our kids to know who is who and to call people by the correct "he" or "she" pronouns.

My 4-year-old son, Adam, had a hard time with gender pronouns. For at least six months, he'd get it backward nearly every time. He'd refer to his female preschool teacher as "he" and say "yes, ma'am" to his dad. We'd correct his usage, but he seemed confused by the rules and was unsure why it all mattered.

But somewhere along the way, it finally clicked. In the last few months, he has become clear on the fact that he is a boy, and his dad is a boy, and his friend Luke is a boy. It was going great until a few weeks ago when I took the boys to lunch at a crowded fast food restaurant, and Adam needed to go to the potty.

I left his 2-year-old brother Jack at the table with the fellow mom I had met for lunch while Adam and I headed for the restrooms. Just as we reached the bathroom door, Adam stopped short.

"Does that say 'MEN'?" he asked, pointing to the men's room door.

"Yes, it does," I answered.

"And this door says 'WOMEN,'" he said.

"Yes, it does. Let's go in," I said as I hurried him through the door.

The ladies room was crowded with women washing hands, chatting and reapplying lipstick. Adam and I slipped into the first stall, but he was becoming more and more anxious.

"I can't go to the woman potty, Mom. I need to go to the man potty," he whispered.

"It's okay, Adam. Boys can go to the women's potty as long as they're with their moms. Let's hurry up so we can get back to the table and eat lunch, okay?"

"No, it's not okay. I can't go pee-pee in the woman potty. I need to go to the man potty like Dad," he said, his voice becoming louder and more distressed.

"Well, Dad is not here right now, Adam, and Mom can't take you into the man potty because that's against the rules. We have to use this potty right now, and next time you can use the man potty with Dad," I explained while I pulled down his jeans and urged him to take care of business.

But at that moment, responding to the call of nature was far less important to Adam than defending his gender identity. Our bathroom negotiations went on for a few more minutes before I finally lost patience and issued a stern mommy mandate: "Adam, you use this potty right now! No more arguing."

Finally, the pee-pee flowed but so did the tears. Between sobs, he wailed his final, futile objection by announcing, "I CAN NOT PEE-PEE IN THIS POTTY! I AM NOT A WOMAN! I AM A MAN!"

I heard muffled chuckling coming from the other stalls, perhaps from fellow mothers who could sympathize with this public bathroom meltdown. I did my best not to laugh with them. Because I realized my son's angst over being emasculated in the Chick-fil-A bathroom was very real, at least for him. So I zipped up his jeans, held him close and assured him that I knew he was right. He was a man. He calmed down a little, and we sprinted out of that woman's potty as fast as we could.

The dramatic bathroom episode has taught me to handle my boy's emerging male ego with care. After all, life is confusing enough for a 4-year-old without someone suddenly bending the gender rules he worked so hard to learn.

Since that day, I've been more careful to make sure everybody goes to our home-based potty before we go out. And I'm constantly on the lookout for one of those public "family" bathrooms, where boys and girls can go potty with either parent in a gender-neutral space.

And if there's not one available, you can bet my husband will be the one chaperoning our sons to the bathroom. After all, a man's gotta do what a man's gotta do.

PREPARING FOR BLAST-OFF

The day before launch:

All day I've had this uncomfortable feeling – the kind that hovers over your head when something big is about to happen. Tomorrow is Adam's first day of kindergarten. He's going to be fine. It's me I'm worried about.

I know I won't be the first woman to have a maternal meltdown after dropping her kid off at school for the first time. I'm sure millions of kindergarten mothers all over the world experience anxiety. But this anticipation mingled with nervousness is killing me right now. I feel like we're in the middle of a slow countdown.

10...9...8...

At the end of the countdown, my little boy – my first baby – will leave the security of our home base and blast off into outer space, otherwise known as public school.

The good news is Adam could not be more excited about the adventure. He has announced to everyone we know, as well as several people we don't, that he is going to kindergarten. He's 5 years old – a certified big boy – and he is in the big leagues now.

My brain tells me he's ready. His preschool teacher confirmed it. He's ready. So why do I have this incredible urge to lock him in a bear hug and not let go? Isn't he supposed to be the one with separation anxiety?

I feel as though tomorrow morning I'll have to rip out my heart, hand it over to the teacher and say, "Here you go. Take good care of this until 2:45 when I come back to pick it up, okay?"

Yes, I know how melodramatic that sounds. And yet I can't get these nagging questions out of my head: What if he gets lost in that maze of unfamiliar hallways? What if his teacher doesn't recognize his "I've got to pee-pee" dance? What if the kid next to him is mean? What if he's scared? What if he runs with scissors? What if he misses me?

...7...6...5...

T minus 2 hours, 15 minutes:

It's morning on the first day of kindergarten. I had no trouble getting out of bed early. I was too nervous to sleep. I keep wondering if there might be a way for me to crawl into Adam's pocket and travel with him into deep space. That way I could pop out just in case he needs me to slay hostile aliens in the cafeteria. The school is only eight minutes from my driveway, so why does it feel like he's going to a galaxy far, far away?

When I woke Adam, he sat up right away, quickly climbed out of bed and said "Time for breakfast!" I made him a pre-launch checklist last night so he was focused on checking off all the items on the list so he could go to school. I videotaped him eating breakfast, brushing his teeth, getting dressed and combing his hair. He was full of energy and all smiles. With backpack and lunchbox in hand, he climbed into the rocket – I mean minivan – and buckled up.

Tom drove us to school so I could snap pictures during drop-off. On the way, we got stuck at a long red light, and I fidgeted nervously as I willed the light to never turn green.

"Mom, are you scared?" Adam asked.

As hard as I was trying to appear calm and collected, my little astronaut could feel the tension welling up inside me. I assured him I wasn't scared at all and just wanted to be sure he was on time for school. The light turned green.

...4...3...2...1...

<u>BLAST-OFF</u>

After reminding him for the fifth time to use his good manners and to have fun, I hugged Adam twice and he gave me the thumbs-up sign. His dad and I walked away from the launch pad, hoping we've prepared him for space exploration.

The tears came during the drive back home, as I knew they would. Tom patted my leg and told me I'd be okay and so would Adam. It's good that I have 3-year-old Jack and 8-month-old Kate to keep me busy today. I need to enjoy this time with them before they get old enough to blast off, too.

Back home, I scooped up the baby and glanced at the clock. In seven hours, the boy explorer will re-enter the home's atmosphere. I can hardly wait to hear about the adventure.

Why Girls Are Gross and Moms Are Okay

On our way home from school each day, we pass a big wooden sign advertising a new shopping center that's coming soon. Just above the "now leasing" banner, there are several silhouettes of women in high heels with long hair, large purses and shopping bags dangling from their delicate wrists. One day last week, as we zipped past the familiar sign, 6-year-old Adam made a pronouncement:

"I don't like that sign," he said.

"What's wrong with that sign?" I asked.

"It's got girls on it," he said. "I don't like girls."

"Really? Why don't you like girls?" I asked.

"Because they're yucky, kind of," he answered.

"Oh," I said. "Did you know that I'm a girl?"

"No, you're not a girl," he corrected. "You're a mom. Moms are womans. And womans are okay."

"Oh, I see. I guess that's lucky for me," I said.

That was the end of it. Adam is a boy of few words, but he holds steadfast to his core beliefs – the newest one being "Girls are gross." In the first few months of kindergarten, I'd ask him whom he played with at recess and the answer – about half the time – was a girl. But sometime during the course of the school year, the kids waged a gender war. It's pink versus blue, frilly versus manly, Strawberry Shortcake versus Spiderman. The kids immediately segregate to boys' and girls' tables at lunch time.

Lately when Adam talks about school recess, he recounts the make-believe battles fought by he and his buddies, the Power Rangers, against the forces of evil. The girls are never part of the story and no one ever speaks of the embarrassing pink Power Ranger.

I gained more insight into Adam's rigid stance on girls last weekend during movie night. His little brother Jack picked the movie "Shrek," but Adam flatly refused to see it.

"No, I don't like Shrek," he said. "We can't watch that one."

"Why not?" I asked. "You used to like Shrek. We've seen it a million times."

"I can only watch Shrek 3," he said. "Not Shrek 1 or Shrek 2 because those have kissing in them, and I don't like kissing."

"Oh, I understand," I said. "You don't like it when Shrek and Fiona kiss?"

"Right. Kissing is very kind of yucky," he said. "That's what girls do. They kiss and they get married. I don't want to get married."

"Well, you're not going to get married for a long, long time," I said. "But it's not a bad thing. Did you know that Dad and I are married?"

"Yes, but you didn't do it when I was there," he said. "You got married and then you had a baby and that baby was me."

"Yep, that's how it happened," I said. Then I quickly changed the subject so things wouldn't detour into "Where do babies come from" before I'm ready to answer. We picked a kiss-free movie and started the show.

When Adam squishes up his face in disgust at the girly shopping center sign and ogre kissing scenes, it takes me straight back to second grade when a cute little boy followed me around the playground constantly. He'd just come out of his "girls are gross" phase but I was still staunchly anti-boy. Annoyed by his attention, I spent most of second grade ignoring him.

Fast forward 10 years to my senior English literature class. Sitting in the desk directly behind me was that same, now grown-up boy and I thought I would absolutely die of sorrowful longing if he didn't talk to me after class. He was the farthest thing from gross, and I internally berated myself for ruining my chances with him in second grade.

Some day before I'm ready, Adam will reverse his position and decide that the frilly girls who grossed him out are the same ones he won't be able to stop thinking about. The same ones he'll spend far too much time texting on his cell phone. The same ones he'll take out for dinner and a movie – a kissing movie. And I, his gender-neutral mother, will stand by and remember a much different time – a time when boys were Power Rangers and girls were "very kind of yucky."

FOOD FIGHT

I have a "picky eater." That doesn't mean the kid won't eat. He eats plenty of food when it's served in the form of pizza, chicken nuggets, bologna, yogurt, cereal bars and grilled cheese sandwiches. But that's the extent of Adam's 6-year-old menu. Now and then he'll eat a serving of green beans, when the stars line up just right and I'm able to cook them the exact same way I did last time with absolutely no variation.

Our only saving grace is that the kid loves fruit. If not for that, I'm certain the nutrition police would have already hauled me off to "bad mama" jail. I've tried a whole host of "get him to try new things" tricks.

Logic:	If you eat those peas, they will make you healthy and strong.
Rewards:	If you eat those peas, you'll get some ice cream for dessert.
Threatening:	If you don't eat those peas, you're not going outside to play after dinner.
Bargaining and pay-offs:	I'll give you a penny for every pea you eat.
Pitiful, desperate begging:	Please, please eat two bites of peas because it would make me so very happy.

Yet my kid will not eat the peas or any other new thing – not for logic or rewards or play time or money or even his tortured mother's happiness. Oh, I can hear what you're thinking. The unspoken judgment is so loud it's nearly deafening: "If you'd let that kid get hungry enough, he'd eat peas or anything else you put in front of him."

And that makes perfect sense. But to that argument I say this: Show me a mama who can let her kid get to that degree of hungry (and cranky), and I'll show you a mama who is much tougher than me and 99 percent of other moms.

At the end of the day, before we settle into our nests, moms have a strong need to know that we've poked food into the mouths of our baby birds. If the baby bird's beak won't open for anything other than a grilled cheese sandwich, then so be it.

Since Adam is normal for his height and weight, I'm certain his menu restrictions aren't making him waste away. I worry more about the effect his pickiness will have on him socially. Before sending him to a friend's house to play recently, I had a long talk with Adam about not being rude about other people's food. "If you don't like what someone offers you, don't say it's yucky or that you don't like it. Just say 'no thank you' and that's all. Understand?" He nodded his head. "I understand, Mom."

When his friend's mom dropped him off at home later that day, she delivered this play-date report: "When the boys came into the kitchen for an after-school snack, Adam said, and I quote, 'If I don't like your food, I'm not going to say it's yucky. I'll just say 'No thank you' and that's all. Okay?'" She agreed that it would be okay, and Adam ate grapes. I'm pretty sure she knew he'd been coached.

I have this vision of Adam as a twenty-something wearing a tuxedo and looking dashing at his wedding reception. In this vision, he is seated beside a banquet table full of chicken nuggets, bologna and cheese sandwiches, pepperoni pizza and yogurt cups, and all the wedding guests are staring in silent judgment wondering "Where did his mother go wrong?"

I've probably gone wrong at a number of different parenting crossroads, but I, like so many other parents of picky eaters, am doing the best I can. I'll keep trying to win the food fight, and I'm praying he'll gradually begin to outgrow his choosiness.

In the meantime, we'll be one of those all-American families preparing our Thanksgiving feast with a side of pepperoni pizza and fruit roll-ups. Bon appetit.

NIGHT CRAWLERS

I woke up early this morning to a familiar feeling – an elbow in the middle of my back. I scooted out of its way and turned my head to see who it was connected to. It was Adam, who is now 7. Next to him 5-year-old Jack slept snuggled under Tom's arm.

Like many couples with young kids, Tom and I don't always wake up alone. We start out that way – just the two of us – which is nice. But at some point in the wee hours, at least one and sometimes both of the boys shuffle sleepily into our room.

I imagine our 2-year-old daughter would join the night parade as well, if she could. But we still have a baby gate on her room and she hasn't yet figured out how to open it. On the nights when she stands at the gate and howls in protest, I pick her up and haul her back to bed with me because it's easier than sleeping on the floor beside her crib.

Tom is a light sleeper – the kind who wakes up when someone three counties away coughs at 2 a.m. So he almost always knows when a sleepy-headed visitor shows up at our door. He usually sends them straight back to their rooms, which I'm sure is the grown-up, responsible thing to do.

I, on the other hand, sleep so soundly it looks like a coma. I hear nothing – not a thunder clap, not a howling wind and certainly not the pitter-pat of socked feet on the bedroom carpet. So the kids have learned through trial and error that, if they can clear the doorway without Dad waking up, they're better off creeping around to my side of the bed. Chances are, I won't wake up when they stealthily crawl onto the bed and worm their way under the covers beside me. Most of the time I don't even know someone is there until I feel the familiar pointy elbow between my shoulder blades. On the off chance I do wake up, they know I'm a sucker for a sleepy kid in pajamas who needs a snuggle to get back to sleep. So I make room for them on my side of the bed.

Of course, it's much more comfortable on the nights when they manage to stay in their own rooms until morning. Even though our bed is king size, it fills up fast with little kids who sprawl out in their sleep and turn sideways and kick off covers. Some nights I wake up to find that I'm clinging to the last two inches on the edge of the bed, wondering how people so little can take up so much space.

It doesn't matter how many times I scoot a kid toward the center of the bed so I can have more room, because kids are like heat-seeking missiles. Even unconscious, they gravitate to their mother's warmth and stick like Velcro.

Despite the lack of space and all the squirming around, I still secretly love these moments. I'm never more content than when I'm nestled in with my sleeping kids sandwiched safely between me and Tom. The house is still and dark, and the only sounds are those of their soft snoring. It's so peaceful, and it feels like our bed is full of blessings.

During those quiet moments, my mind flashes back to a memory of a cat we had when I was growing up. She was an outdoor calico cat we named "Callie." My dad always called her "the cat factory" because it seemed like she was having kittens every other week. I loved every new batch of kittens and spent lots of time watching them in the cardboard box maternity ward we always fixed up for her.

The kittens would nurse and fall asleep still nuzzled against their mother's warm belly, and Callie would get this certain look on her face. I know cats can't technically smile, but this look came pretty close. It was almost like she was drunk on the perfect cocktail of peace, love and contentment. She was in bliss – pure, maternal bliss in its truest form.

During those quiet nights in my king size bed crowded with little knees and elbows, I think I understand how she felt.

So I'm going to treasure these nights because I know that one day there won't be any kids in dinosaur pajamas tiptoeing into our room at night. They'll grow up. They'll become "too cool." They won't sleep in the bend of my arm the way they did when they were babies. There won't be any more Saturday morning snuggles under the covers while cartoons play on TV.

I'll have plenty of years to sprawl out in bed and hog the covers when they're teenagers and can't be bothered with their ancient mother. But for now, I hold them close, like a mama cat purring with her babies. Because for now, they're all mine.

Sweet dreams.

Two Points

When Adam said he wanted to be on a basketball team, I was happy. There's a sport I can not only understand but also enjoy from the relative comfort of nearby indoor bleachers. And whoever invented basketball had the good sense to end the game after four periods instead of nine innings. In basketball, helmeted linebackers don't run full-speed at my first-grader with the sole intention of squashing him into the dirt. Mamas like that.

Adam joined the church-based basketball league and could hardly wait to wear his jersey. The team practiced for a few weeks before the games began, and Tom served as assistant coach. He said Adam was doing pretty well with shooting, so I guess all those games of horse on the driveway were paying off.

Then it was game time. With my video camera at the ready, the buzzer sounded and the game began. I'd already promised myself I wasn't going to be one of those crazy parents who can't shut up on the sidelines. But five minutes into the game, I realized how tough it is to watch quietly.

From my vantage point, it was easy to see that he just needed to guard his man a little more, rebound the basketball and get in position to shoot. I wanted to yell all these things to him to help him out. But after a few minutes of fruitless sideline instruction, I knew I wasn't helping anything except my own need to point him in the right direction. The boys had all they could handle just trying to remember which goal was theirs and to hear directions from the coach over the noise of an echo-chamber gym filled with parents all "trying to help."

Then something happened that got me on my feet. My boy had the ball in heavy traffic. Trying desperately to get a shot in the air, he was mauled by a taller boy trying to steal the ball. Adam fell to the floor where a shoe or two accidentally stepped down on him amidst the scramble. I could see the pain and frustration on his face. The mama bear in me wanted to rush the court, break up the gaggle of boys and scoop mine up in my arms. I wanted to march that defensive player right over to a naughty corner and give him a lengthy time-out and a piece of my mind.

But the rational part of me stayed put because rescuing him as if he was a baby was not going to earn him any "cool points." So I let the referee do his job, and Adam brushed himself off and shot two free-throws, one of which went in the net.

After the game, he was happy about making that free-throw, but his heart yearned for a real basket – one shot in the heat of battle, one that swishes through the net, just like it does on the Sports Center highlights he watches every morning before school.

About midway through the game schedule, Adam still hadn't made that elusive shot, and, one day after practice, he crumbled under the weight of his own expectations. As we drove home, I heard him mumbling in the backseat. "I'm never gonna make a basket. Never, ever, ever. I'll never make a basket."

I told him that if he kept on practicing and trying his best, it would happen one day. I gave him the speech about believing in yourself and

never giving up, but the words fell flat. He just wanted that basket, and it wasn't happening.

Fast forward four days to the next big game on Saturday afternoon. It was late in the third quarter, and a teammate had just passed the ball to Adam at mid-court. I could see the determination in his eyes, and there was no way he was letting go of that ball until he'd taken his shot.

He dribbled down the court into traffic, pushing his way closer to the goal. He picked up the dribble and bent his knees, preparing to shoot. Suddenly time slowed down, and I was able to say several prayers in a row as the ball went into the air: "Please let it go in. Please, please, please go in."

But the ball hit the rim hard and bounced off. My heart fell and my head dropped. When I looked up, there he was with the ball again! He'd somehow captured his own rebound and dribbled to the other side of the court where he shot the ball a second time. More praying, more holding my breath, more throat-constricting anxiety – then swish! It dropped through the net gracefully. Two points!

I immediately stood up and screamed a triumphant scream of joy that may have damaged the hearing of the guy sitting in front of me. But I couldn't help myself. My son had made his first real basket! I looked over at his dad who was cheering from the coach's bench with the other players.

When Adam finally glanced my way to see if I saw his shot, I waved my arm wildly like a dorky sideline lunatic. I gave him a cheesy thumbs-up sign, and he flashed the same sign back at me.

After the game, we drove home reliving that play over and over again – doing color commentary the way the ESPN guys do. Adam couldn't stop smiling and neither could I. I'd just watched him learn that, with the right amount of effort and patience, nearly anything is possible – even two points.

ONE DECADE LATER

I have a big birthday coming up. And I'll be the first to admit it's freaking me out. My oldest child is turning 10. As in 10 years old. Double digits. This is huge. Staring my own middle age in the face doesn't seem nearly as tough as knowing that the snuggly baby who used to sleep on my shoulder is about to mark his first decade of life.

How did this happen? I know it sounds cliché but it really does seem like we were videotaping his first few wobbly steps just a few years ago. And now it feels like he's sprinting away from me, determined to grow up and chase his own adventures.

Last night at the kids' bedtime, I watched Adam walk away from me, down the hallway toward his room. He was wearing pajama bottoms but no shirt. And suddenly I got this pang of sadness way down deep in my gut because I realized he doesn't look much like a little kid anymore. He's somewhere between kid and lean, gangly teenager, and it's becoming clear that he's picking up speed on this onramp to full-fledged adolescence.

One of the only things that hasn't changed about him during these past 10 years is his sleepwalking. He did it back when he was still wearing footed-pajamas and he does it now. But these days, if he sleepwalks to our bed in the middle of the night, I can't just scoop him up like a sack of potatoes, the way I did when he was 3. He has grown into a 70-pound sack of potatoes.

When Tom and I try to pick him up and move him, he's all legs and arms and elbows pointing out in every direction, and one of us will likely throw out our back one of these nights trying to prove to ourselves that he's still our baby.

One of the things bothering Tom most about this 10-year mark is knowing that, in just six years, Adam will be driving. Not a scooter, not a bicycle. A two-ton car capable of high rates of speed. I shudder even typing those words.

But the thing that gets me most – the thing that makes the tears well up in my eyes and my throat constrict – is knowing that the 18 years we'll have him at home is more than half over. And if the first 10 years went this quickly, the next eight will also fly.

Despite all the parental angst, I do understand the thrill this new phase of life brings with it. A decade ago I was worrying about colic, croup and if he'd start crawling when all the baby books said he should.

Today that same person is making his own bologna and cheese sandwiches. He's kind, polite and funny. He's a voracious reader whose constant quest to know more makes us proud. We marvel at the person he's becoming.

So happy birthday, my boy. If you see my eyes get watery when you blow out your candles, just know that it's not because I'm sad. It's because I'm sad, happy, proud, scared, amazed and nervous all at the same time. None of it makes any sense to you, I know. But it will one day – when your firstborn turns 10.

Dream Big and Pack a Sharpie

Often the best conversations I have with my kids happen on the way to somewhere. I don't remember what errand we were running when my son Adam and I had this exchange, but I'll remember the talk for a long time.

Him: "Mom, I've decided to write a bucket list. You know what a bucket list is?"

Me: "Yes, it's a list of things you want to do before you die. You do realize you're only 10 years old, right?"

Him: "Yeah, I know. I just think it'll be good to have a list."

Me: "You're right. So what are you gonna put on your bucket list?"

Him: "Well, the first thing is 'Be on a game show.' Either Kids Jeopardy or Wheel of Fortune."

Me: "Excellent choice. What else is going on the list?"

Him: "I also want to write my name on the moon with a Sharpie."

Me: (Stunned silence.) "Uh, okay... That's pretty interesting. So does this mean you're going to be an astronaut and go into outer space? Did you change your mind about playing in the NBA for the Chicago Bulls and being an announcer for ESPN?"

Him: "No, I didn't change my mind about that. I definitely want to do those things, too."

Me: "Oh. Wow. So you're going to play for the NBA, be a sports announcer AND become an astronaut?"

Him: (Noting the skepticism in my question) "So I can't do all those things? Is that too much? Maybe I should mark the moon off the list."

As he thought about scaling back, I remembered something I saw online recently – a quote from an unknown source that says, "Have big dreams. You will grow into them."

And it reminded me that I should never imply that my kid's dreams might be too much or too big. Because I don't know what he'll grow into. Who knows what possibilities may exist for his generation? Perhaps by then people will be taking quick sightseeing adventures to the moon the same way we rent a hotel room in Branson for the weekend. So I retracted my earlier skepticism.

Me: "Actually, I bet you can do all those things. Who knows what you'll do when you're a grown-up? And you shouldn't take things off your list. If you want to do them, then they should go on the list. Your bucket list can have all kinds of cool dreams on it."

Him: "Good. Because it would be really cool to write my name on the moon."

Me: "Definitely. I'd have never even thought of something that cool. And it's smart to use a Sharpie marker because then the ink won't wear off."

He smiled and nodded, and then we moved on to other important matters like whether or not we could have pizza for dinner.

But that conversation has stayed with me – reminding me how important it is to reach for something that forces us to grow. As adults, we often compress big dreams down into more practical packages. We edit them down so small that they disappear or become something that looks more like a mundane to-do list versus a big-dream bucket list.

I'm realizing now that part of my job as a parent is to protect my kids' ability to dream. I don't have to figure out how they're going to accomplish those dreams. I just have to help them believe in themselves enough so that they're not afraid to try – to "reach for the stars," so to speak, or possibly even autograph the moon.

CHAPTER 3

THE MIDDLE
CHILD FILE

Second Time Around

When the home pregnancy test confirmed it nine months ago, I thought I knew what to expect. I've already been around the pregnancy block once, and I assumed I'd recognize all the scenery the second time around. But now, as I near the prenatal finish line, I realize a second pregnancy can be a completely different trip than the first.

The contrasts were evident from the start. When Adam was in utero two and a half years ago, I had "hit and run" morning sickness. It would hit. Then I'd run to the nearest bathroom. But then it was over. I'd feel fine again and go about my routine until the next time it hit, often days later.

But this pregnancy has felt like being on a boat heading into high seas, with a captain who enjoyed a few too many cocktails before leaving port. Every room seems to sway, and for the first few months I stayed a shade of pukey green nearly 24 hours a day.

During the first pregnancy, there were middle-of-the-night leg cramps that made me want to climb the bedroom curtains and howl in pain. But balancing that out was the perk of being able to eat absolutely anything and everything without even a minute's worth of indigestion.

Photo: AnnaLee Livingston

This time around, there are thankfully no leg cramps tying me in knots, but I could be the poster girl for Tums antacids.

A mother in her second pregnancy definitely gets treated differently, too. When you're a first-timer, people find out you're pregnant and begin handling you like a fragile piece of wedding china. Nobody lets you lift anything heavier than your dinner fork. People cross rooms to hand you the remote control. And your husband will gladly get dressed at 11 p.m. to go out and fetch you a burrito from the Taco Bell drive-through with no remark other than "Want hot or mild sauce with that?"

But once you've survived that first pregnancy and become a mother, you're an entirely different creature. You're a mother now, and mothers are tough, durable. Mothers take care of people, including themselves. Nobody bats an eye when they see a pregnant mother schlepping a 30-pound toddler and three bags of groceries across a parking lot in the rain. You're less like a delicate piece of wedding china and more like a sturdy serving platter.

As for those nights around 11 p.m. when you rub your round tummy and drop hints to your husband for a burrito, the first-timer honeymoon is over by then. He's much more likely to say, "Sure, get me one, too, and put gas in the car while you're out. Don't forget the hot sauce."

But perhaps the biggest difference I've noted between my first pregnancy and this one are these last few days before the due date. With Adam, there was no real sense of waiting for labor to start. Like most first-timers, I expected to have him on his due date or maybe a day or two later. But 11 days before that date, with no real warning signs, I woke up around midnight and realized it was time to go to the hospital. It happened so quickly. One minute I was at the office working on a marketing budget. The next minute I was asking for an epidural and fast.

Because I was caught off guard last time, I'm determined to be more than ready for this baby's arrival. My hospital bag has been packed for weeks. The nursery is ready. Baby clothes are washed and folded. I'm in a constant state of "nesting" – tidying up the house in case tonight is the night. And I've shaved my legs more in the past two weeks than I have in the past two years. Yet, still the baby hasn't come, and the anticipation is building with every false labor pain.

But wait we must because this baby, like the entire pregnancy, is uniquely different and the timing is out of our hands. Pass the burrito… and the Tums.

Today I Laid an Egg

Parenthood is not a glamorous sport. Often it can be downright humbling. Some days, it sneaks a toe over the line into "humiliating." Last Sunday was one of those days.

We got up early with a mission – get ourselves and the two boys dressed and ready for church. We'd been shamefully absent from Sunday services in the few months since the new baby arrived, and we vowed to do better.

So after breakfast and diaper changes, Tom dressed 2-year-old Adam while I dressed the baby. Then I packed his diaper bag with extra changes of clothes for both kids, so I'd be prepared for a leaky diaper or spilled drink. After all, a smart mother has to plan ahead for mishaps.

Then I began searching for something to wear. I hadn't worn anything but stretchy pants and t-shirts since Jack was born, so I had to dig way back into the guest room closet to find the light beige, dressy pants I'd worn more than a year earlier. I found them and put them on, praying they'd fit again. I had to suck in hard and remove a couple ribs, but I got them buttoned. Then I chose a silk, button-up shirt and emerged from the closet looking more put together than I had in a long time – nice clothes, wrinkle and spit-up free.

Church was great, and neither kid cried. Afterward, we headed to a nice restaurant to meet friends for lunch. Once we parked, I climbed into the backseat, brushed aside several toddler toys, and sat between the two carseats to feed the baby.

Once Jack was fed, burped and back in his infant seat, we all got out and headed for the restaurant door. I led the way with Adam, and Tom followed behind carrying the baby. Our friends hadn't arrived yet, so we asked for a large table to accommodate four adults and two kids. The hostess led us all the way through the large, crowded restaurant and finally stopped at a booth near the back.

I was just about to sit down when a waitress leaned over to me and said in a hushed voice, "Ma'am, you've got something hanging off your behind. I think it may be Silly Putty."

I reached behind me and, to my horror, felt a melted, gooey mess as well as half of the Silly Putty egg that the goo had come out of. Even worse, it was blue Silly Putty on light beige pants. It practically screamed for attention.

It was one of those moments when you wish for the Earth to instantly open up and swallow you whole. I had just traipsed through one of the nicest restaurants in town in front of a capacity crowd with a blue gob of Silly Putty and a plastic egg dangling from my butt.

If only we'd been at McDonald's or Chuck E. Cheese, it wouldn't have been nearly as embarrassing. At those kinds of places, it's not all that uncommon to see an oblivious mother with random objects stuck to her butt. But this was no McDonald's. This was the kind of place where the napkins are linen and the patrons don't wear Silly Putty.

I tried in vain to scrape off the melted putty, but it was no use. If my butt had been a car, it was totaled. A complete loss. Inside the diaper bag were extra clothes for the kids, but there was nothing for me. I hadn't anticipated being the one wearing the mess. After lunch, during the long walk out of the restaurant, I held the diaper bag over my behind and ordered Tom to follow close behind.

On the drive home, I berated him for not noticing the blue egg on my butt before the waitress spotted it. "I was carrying the baby," he said. "How was I supposed to know I should be looking for an egg hanging from your rear?"

I fired back, saying, "I bet you would've noticed if Jennifer Lopez walked in front of you with a Silly Putty egg on her butt!"

"Maybe so," he teased, "but then again I don't see her butt every day."

Needless to say, this was not the right response. (Note to husbands everywhere: When your wife has just been seen in public with blue goo and a plastic egg on her butt, do not say anything which might imply that hers is also an old, familiar butt.)

Despite my humiliation, I did learn a few things that might prevent this type of social tragedy in the future.

No. 1: Never let your kid play with Silly Putty in the car.
No. 2: Check your rear before walking through a fancy restaurant.
No. 3: Pack some mishap clothes of your own.

You never know when you might be the one who accidentally lays an egg.

Naked Nuggets

Everyone said it would be easier this time. Potty-training kid No. 2 is supposed to be a snap because kid No. 2 is so eager to emulate the potty skills of kid No. 1. There's a built-in motivation to be a "big boy." And parents have gained some wisdom and confidence because they've already done time in the potty-training trenches and lived to tell about it.

I wasn't worried about Jack's transition from diapers to potty. I knew it would happen, one way or another. I bought him his own training potty more than a year ago, hoping he might be inspired to ditch the diapers before his little sister was born. Jack loved the new little potty and was happy to sit on it and show off his deposit. But time passed and the novelty wore off. Jack lost interest and abandoned the bathroom altogether.

So I backed off, partly because that's what all the potty-training books tell you to do but mostly because I was five months pregnant at the time and didn't have the energy to force the issue. I decided to wait until after the baby was born and pray there'd be another window of opportunity. That was 10 months ago.

Finally that proverbial window cracked open. One day Jack announced he was going to the potty. He rounded the corner into the bathroom and insisted on privacy. After he was done, I offered him a choice: diaper or underwear. He reached out for the Scooby Doo underwear, pulled them on and that was it. He showed them off proudly to his older brother. He had officially joined the ranks of the big boys.

Jack had his share of accidents at first and would announce them by telling me he "peeped" in his pants. I taught him to take off his wet underwear, put it in the laundry basket and get a clean pair out of the drawer. By the end of the week, he was dry all day. Ah, sweet victory was mine! Two of my three kids were out of diapers. I decided to take the kids to Chick-fil-A for a celebratory lunch.

The boys scarfed down their meals and ran off to play in the indoor play area. Seated in a nearby booth, I watched them through the plexiglass window and marveled at how quickly my first two babies had become independent little boys. I sat there leisurely enjoying my lunch, congratulating myself on my superior potty-training skills. Truly, it had been easier the second time around.

Then the god of "Not So Fast" paid me a cruel visit. I glanced over toward the play area to check on the boys and saw a scene that will forever be burned in my memory. There was Jack – standing in the middle of the play area completely nude from the waist down. The entire restaurant was getting a full moon, and there was a group of wide-eyed little girls standing in front of him staring down at his naked nuggets.

I bolted from my booth and raced into the play area. "Jack!" I yelled. "What are you doing?" He looked up at me and then pointed toward a pile of soggy underwear and shorts near the bottom of the slide. "Mom, I peeped on Scooby Doo," he explained. I scooped them up and hurriedly put them back on him. "Jack, we don't take our clothes off in

Chick-fil-A!" Then I did what any mother would do in this situation. I made a break for it.

I rushed my crew out and sprinted toward the minivan, hoping to escape the embarrassment of the lunchtime striptease. I can only imagine the questions those little girls had for their mothers after I hustled my little flasher out of there.

After we got home, I had a long talk with Jack about when it is and is NOT appropriate to take off one's soggy Scooby Doo underwear. I can only hope he'll remember the guidelines. Then I took an Advil, collapsed on the sofa and tried to reassure myself that this kind of thing probably happens to everyone. Parenting, at any stage, is full of surprises – even the second time around.

THE SOUND OF SILENCE

When I was a little girl, my mother and I had a tradition. On a special night in September, she'd cook popcorn on the stove, make Coke floats and we'd settle in on the sofa to watch the Miss America pageant. It was just the two of us because nothing made my brother and father scatter faster than a televised beauty pageant.

For Mom, this was serious business. She watched the pageant with a notebook and pen in hand, jotting down her predictions for the top ten and crossing through the name of the poor girl who stumbled in her high heels. We'd root for our state's contestant, and, if she didn't make the Top Ten, we'd root for whoever had the best talent, the prettiest evening gown and managed to answer the interview question without sounding like Betty Boop.

Lately I've been reminiscing about those pageant nights, and one burning question keeps coming to mind: What happened to the isolation booth? I really, really need to know.

The isolation booth was a glass-paneled box wheeled onto stage when it was time for the interview portion of the pageant. Four of the top five contestants would be ushered through the door of the booth where they'd all wait their turn to come out, step up to the emcee's microphone and answer the tough question.

While the first contestant answered, the rest of the girls would stand in the booth with their big hair and smile vacantly because they couldn't hear a thing. That's the beauty of the isolation booth. Completely soundproof. It wouldn't have mattered if Bert Parks shouted "FIRE, FIRE! RUN FOR YOUR LIVES!" Those girls would have stood there serenely on their island of silence.

Over the years, the pageant evolved. They retired the isolation booth and each contestant had to answer a different question. But there are many days when I wonder what may have happened to that old relic. Where is it now? More importantly, can I have it? Please?

I know an isolation booth might look a little strange in our living room, but I need it. It's the kids, you see. They're LOUD. I love these little people, and I nearly turned a cartwheel when the boys said their first words. I couldn't wait until we could have real conversations. But now they are 5 and 3 years old, and they know A LOT of words, which they put together to form A LOT of questions. Here's a typical snippet of our conversation:

"Mom, can you get me some chocolate milk?"

"Where is the chocolate milk, Mom? Mom, did you get some at the store?"

"Can I go to the store with you, Mom?"

"When we go to the store, can I get that Spiderman that crawls up the walls and shoots the webs out like this?" (Boy imitates superhero by crawling up kitchen island and then falls off due to lack of web-spinning ability.)

"Owwww! Mom, oh, I hurt my elbow. Is my elbow bleeding, Mom? Can you look at it? Mom, I need a Band-Aid. Can you get me a Band-

Aid, Mom? Mom, can you put one of those Spiderman Band-Aids on it, okay? (Mom applies Band-aid.)

"Oh, good. That's better. I like Spiderman Band-Aids. Mom, can you get me some chocolate milk?"

Now I love my two boys like crazy, but there are days when the constant barrage of questions and requests – not to mention the background noise of cartoon theme songs and the endless sound effects boys make while playing with racecars – makes me want to press my hands over my ears and run screaming into traffic.

Those are the days when I wistfully long for my own isolation booth. If I could just go in there for 15 or 20 minutes a day and lock the door, I could soak in that beautiful silence and hear myself think for a while. I'd still be able to see the boys, but I wouldn't hear a thing. I'd just stand there and smile serenely and give them a pageant wave from behind the heavy glass walls. Oh, that booth could do wonders.

I know that thing is probably sitting in some dusty storage building somewhere in Atlantic City, never again to be filled with beauties in sequined evening gowns. I'm no Miss America, but I sure could put that booth to good use.

I'd even pay the FedEx charges to get it here. Just a few minutes a day in the glassy silence, and I'm sure I'd come out with all the answers to the really tough questions about chocolate milk and Spiderman Band-Aids and world peace.

Yakety-yak, Mom Looks Back

It happened, as I knew it would. Last Friday I waited in the line of cars and mini-vans outside the boys' elementary school. When my kids' names were called, I peered out the window to watch them run out the double-doors. But on that day, something was distinctly different about the typically joyful exit. While Adam was jogging happily toward the van, Jack was trudging slowly with his head down.

"Ah," I thought to myself. "It happened today."

The boys climbed into the van – first Adam and then his downcast little brother. Jack, who is usually bubbling over with information about his day in kindergarten, was very quiet which confirmed my suspicion.

"Mom, Jack has something to tell you today," Adam said in a sing-song manner that showed he was enjoying this way too much.

"What is it, Jack?" I said, playing dumb.

"I don't want to talk about it," he said quietly.

"It's okay, Jack. You can tell me," I said.

"I changed my stoplight to yellow today," he confessed.

He handed me a slip of paper bearing a frowning face that said Jack had received an official warning from his teacher for "talking too much."

Jack's older brother, Adam, was smiling broadly because he, too, had earned a few yellow warning lights during his kindergarten year and he certainly didn't want to be outdone by his little brother. I shot Adam "the look" so he wouldn't compound Jack's misery.

"Jack, it's okay. Everybody makes mistakes. You just have to try not to make the same mistake again."

As we drove out of the parking lot, I glanced down at the warning slip again and smiled secretly at the words "talking too much." This was not a mistake I would've ever made in school – not because I didn't want to, but because I couldn't. Unlike Jack, I had a paralyzing shyness that dictated so much of what I did and didn't do throughout my childhood. It robbed me of some of the fun I should have had, friends I might have made.

I was that little kid hiding behind her mother's legs. I remember desperately wanting to answer questions in class as I got older but not having the guts to raise my hand. As a teenager, I didn't date until I was nearly 18 – not because I didn't want to, but because talking to a boy felt like jumping off a cliff.

Eventually, shyness led me to writing because, on paper, I was set free. I wanted that same freedom in real life so, in college, during a rare moment of bravery, I signed up for a public speaking course. It terrified me but it also forced me to practice. Then I took a bank teller job that made me have short conversations with customers all day long. It was brutal at first, but it got easier.

Ironically, I ended up as a reporter in my early 20s and learned how to interview strangers and write about them. It wasn't just a job. For a shy girl like me, it was also therapy.

But my boy Jack won't have to work that hard because he is naturally outgoing and loves to talk. He's the kid in the park who runs up to other kids and asks if they want to play. He's warm and engaging, and I marvel at how easily he makes friends. How did someone like him come from someone like me? The gene pool is a funny, wonderful thing sometimes.

As we pulled into our driveway, I told Jack to work extra hard on not talking when the teacher asks him to be quiet. He nodded that he'd do better.

But I'll admit there's a part of me – a part down deep that's still connected to that shy girl – who is glad and relieved that my little boy has the ability and the confidence to "talk too much."

"I Can Explain…"

Early this morning, I opened my eyes and saw 7-year-old Jack's eyes looking right at me, just inches from my face.

"Mom," he whispered. "I need to tell you something."

"What is it, Jack?" I groaned sleepily.

"The tooth fairy didn't come last night," he said. "My tooth is still there under the pillow and there's no money!"

I bolted upright in the bed with a sick feeling in the pit of my stomach. Mommy guilt flooded through me instantly. I'd forgotten about the tooth fairy's scheduled visit. Jack's wiggly tooth had fallen out early in the day and was a distant memory by the time I finally fell into bed the night before.

"Oh, really?" I said, desperately trying to think of a way to fix this. "I wonder what could have happened."

Then, proving once again that I married well, Tom rolled over in bed and said groggily, "Jack, I bet the Tooth Fairy is just running late because of the snow. She'll probably come while you're at school today."

"Oh! Okay, that makes sense," Jack said. "I'll just check when I get home from school."

Jack went downstairs to eat breakfast and watch for signs of the Tooth Fairy flying through the light snowfall outside the kitchen window. I thanked God for winter precipitation and then congratulated Tom on his quick thinking at such an early hour. I can think on my feet but not before 7 a.m. and definitely not before a cup of caffeine.

This wasn't our first close call. A few years ago, I got caught in a Christmas situation that required fancy footwork. Late one night I'd wrapped all the kids' gifts and put them under the tree, but I'd forgotten to hide the ones that were marked "From Santa." The next day, Adam (who was by then able to read), noticed the tags and asked me how come there was a gift under the tree from Santa, since Santa only comes on Christmas Eve.

With as much conviction as I could muster, I explained that Santa's sleigh isn't big enough to carry all the gifts for all the children in the world at the same time. So sometimes he has to send the gifts to your house a few weeks early.

"But how does Santa get them here?" Adam asked.

"Fed Ex," I said.

And that's why, to this day, my kids are thrilled any time they see the Fed Ex truck in our neighborhood, hoping that, even though it's February, perhaps Santa is sending them another really early Christmas gift.

That's the thing about parenting. It requires us to make judgment calls about whether it's more important to tell the whole truth and nothing but the truth, or if – in some cases – it's better to protect your kids' sense of childhood magic and wonder. When does the Tooth Fairy hang up her wings? When does Santa stop using Fed Ex? How does the Easter Bunny get off the bunny trail?

Sometimes I worry that one day – when the kids start piecing together the facts – we'll have to come clean about all these creative explanations we've shared over the years. Will it take the sparkle out of their eyes? Will they become jaded and disillusioned? Will they wonder if they've been raised by pathological liars?

I hope not. I hope they forgive us our fibs of affection. And I really hope they don't adopt "creative explanations" themselves when they become teenagers and need to get out of a jam of their own.

SOCK IT TO ME

There's an old TV commercial for Tootsie Pops featuring a cartoon boy who poses this question to wise Mr. Owl: "How many licks does it take to get to the Tootsie Roll center of a Tootsie Pop?" The owl replies "Let's find out," as he takes the little boy's Tootsie Pop and begins licking and counting aloud.

At my house, there's a similar experiment underway. Adam and Jack are on a quest to find out how many socks it takes to make their mother insane. Last night, they came dangerously close to witnessing a full-blown trip to Crazytown.

I know it shouldn't bother me this much. They're socks – not landmines. But what started as a pet peeve grew into a frustration and has now morphed into a trigger. For some moms, it's dirty dishes left behind on the counter or globs of toothpaste cemented onto the bathroom sink. But every mama has something that drives her a little nuts, and, for me, it's the socks.

Since they were toddlers, I've always been able to track the boys by following a trail of socks. At the end of the trail, I'd find two barefoot brothers oblivious to why I might be irritated. I figured the best way to teach them was to make them pick up their own socks and put them in the hamper. I was sure they'd eventually learn that it's easier to put the socks in the hamper before I started to hassle them about it.

But we've been doing this forced march to the hamper for YEARS now. And yet, still, I find socks. Everywhere. Inside-out, balled-up socks – in the kitchen, by the front door, in the hallway, under tables, under bed covers. The endless repetition of "Put your socks in the hamper!" has nearly driven me mad.

Last night, after I'd spent the better part of the day getting the house in order, I walked into the living room to watch TV with the kids. As I began to sit down, I stopped short. There, in the very spot I was about to sit, were two discarded socks – the same two socks that broke the proverbial camel's back.

"WHO left their socks here?" I yelled at the boys as I pointed toward the offending footwear. My tone and volume told them this was serious.

"They're HIS!" they both said in unison, each brother pointing at the other.

"How many times do I have to say the exact same thing?" I yelled, continuing my rant. "What part of 'Put your socks away' do you NOT understand? Do you think I was put on this Earth to pick up socks every single day of my life? Do you? Well, I wasn't!"

They both stood there stunned, shocked that socks could have triggered such a maternal meltdown. They'd accidentally opened a big ol' can of crazy and desperately wanted to stuff it back in.

"You guys better get these socks out of my sight and into the hamper in the next 10 seconds or you do NOT want to know what'll happen," I threatened.

Honestly, even I didn't know what would happen, but I knew none of us wanted to see things get uglier. In less than a second, they'd each grabbed a sock and sprinted upstairs toward the hamper and away from the nuclear reactor that was once their mother.

So how many strewn-around socks does it take to make your mother crazy? I'm not sure. But I do know this. You don't want to find out.

Letter to My Middle Child

Dear Jack,

Eight years ago tonight, we met for the first time. I was the exhausted woman with the lovely epidural drip. You were the very red, very loud newborn who came roaring into the room at 11 p.m. You fit into my arms like a puzzle piece, and I marveled at your perfect skin and wavy hair.

Your brother didn't warm up to you as instantly as Dad and I did. He ignored you those first few months because he was only 2 years old and unimpressed when you came home and did nothing but eat, sleep and spit up on people. But one day, after several months of taking no notice of you, he walked by the baby swing where you were nestled and reached out to pat you gently on the head. You smiled up at him. After that, you were "in." He couldn't deny your charm.

Speaking of charm, you've always had plenty. Sure, you had your share of toddler temper tantrums, but you also had an irresistible twinkle in your eyes that made even the most trying days manageable.

One spring you fell in love with a pair of green rubber rain boots with alligators on them. Because you were the second child, I'd learned to pick my battles and footwear didn't make the list. So I let you wear your beloved rain boots everywhere. And people would stop to comment on your cute boots, which made you beam and love them all the more.

But I don't think it was the boots that turned heads. It was the way you wore them with such a natural swagger. Not everyone is cool enough to make rubber boots look cool, but you did.

When you started preschool, I didn't worry because you already had an easy way with people. Every time I see you in action, I wonder how someone as outgoing as you came from someone like me. You're the kid who makes friends everywhere he goes. One of these days, you should teach me how you do it.

I dropped you off at a friend's birthday party a few weeks ago, and when you walked through the door, four boys yelled your name and rushed to meet you with hugs and high fives. I felt like the mother of a little rock star.

But your magnetic personality isn't what I love most about you. It's your heart. Oh boy, is it big. It makes mine swell with pride every time I think of all the times I've watched you put your own wishes aside in order to make someone else happy. You do it instinctively, so I know God must have made you this way.

I never put much stock in birth order stereotypes, but seeing how you broker peace treaties between an older brother and younger sister has made me think maybe there's something to it after all. You're the

creamy white filling between rigid sibling cookies. You make it work, and they love you for it.

You play one-on-one basketball with your brother and easily transition into playing make-believe with your little sister, and you're somehow equally happy doing both.

They say the middle child often gets overlooked, and I hope we never make you feel that way. You deserve attention, and I want you to feel as special as you are.

So happy eighth birthday, Jack. I'm immensely proud of the person you've been ever since you came roaring into my hospital room. And I'm blessed to have this front row seat to watch where you and your tender heart go from here.

CHAPTER 4

THE GIRL CHILD
FILE

THIRD TIME AROUND

The day before Easter, I paced around the bathroom floor for exactly three minutes. Then I peeked over at the little white test stick on the counter and read the result – positive. Baby No. 3 was officially on the way.

I wasn't completely surprised by the tell-tale line on the home pregnancy test. Days before taking the test, I felt a heavy fatigue that compelled me to take naps with our 2-year-old. It's normal for a mom of two young boys to feel tired, but there's something undeniably different about the hormonally-induced coma-type sleep that early pregnancy brings.

The great thing about carrying a third child is knowing much of what to expect – the fatigue, the excitement, the extra trips to the bathroom. The surprising thing about carrying a third child is how often you're still surprised. That's the thing about miracles – no two are ever quite the same.

The first trimester was bumpy, as we weathered a few health scares. But after almost four months of close monitoring by my doctor, everything looks good. As for feeling good, that's a different story. Much to my surprise, this pregnancy served up a lingering morning sickness that lasted well into the fifth month. But a little time and a great nausea medication finally cured that problem, which brings me to where I am today – heading into the homestretch third trimester and looking forward to a Christmas Eve due date.

When it's your third time around, your poor abdominal muscles don't even put up a decent fight. It's as if they sense the presence of that tiny fetus and give way long before it's time to be "showing." I wasn't even out of the first trimester before I was out of my regular jeans and searching the back of my closet for those maternity pants with the stretchy belly panel.

Now I'm smack in the middle of the waddling around stage, and friends have been asking how our sons – who are now 5 and 2 – are feeling about the upcoming family addition.

Their response to the news was as different as the boys themselves. Two-year-old Jack was the first to point to my swelling belly, as if to point out to me that it was bigger than usual. I told him there was a baby in my belly and that he would be a big brother one day. He smiled, patted my belly and said "baby." Ten seconds later, he lifted his own shirt, patted his belly and said "my baby." That's the great thing about 2-year-olds. If Mom or Dad says it, it must be true. No questions asked.

But our oldest son, Adam, needs things to make sense. He is almost 5, after all, and 5-year-olds want a plausible explanation for the world around them. I told him there was indeed a baby in my belly and that one day Mom and Dad would go to the hospital to pick up the new baby, hoping to avoid the whole "How does the baby get out of there?" conversation.

But Adam dismissed my claim immediately, saying, "There's not a baby in your belly. That's silly." So I turned the tables and asked him to explain it to me. "So if it's not a baby in my belly, then what is it?"

Without even pausing to think, he answered, "A big grilled cheese sandwich." And with that, the new baby conversation was over. I decided it would be best not to insist he believe a baby was in my belly, since – in a 5-year-old's world – the only way for a baby to have gotten inside my belly is if I had eaten it for dinner.

So, for now, we don't make a big fuss over the impending arrival. The concept of time for a preschooler and toddler is fuzzy. Tomorrow is about as far out as they can see. As for me and Tom, we can see clearly that the days are speeding by as the due date approaches. We've got to stock our freezer with casseroles and our nursery with diapers before the big day. In the meantime, I'm enjoying the third trimester and marveling at how wonderful it is to feel the little kicks, nudges and twitches of this precious "grilled cheese sandwich."

Open When You're 15

D_{ear} Kate,

I know it seems strange to be writing you a letter now, seeing as how you're only 1 ½ years old and can barely put two words together. But one day, about 14 years from now, I'll dig this dusty letter out of a box and show it to you so you'll understand what it was like to be your mother when you were only 25 pounds and 31 inches tall.

There's an old rhyme that says boys are made of "snakes and snails and puppy dog tails," while girls are "sugar and spice and everything nice." But I think perhaps a few jalapenos got thrown into the mix when God dreamed you up because you're surprising and intense.

Today is a good example. I was working diligently on my computer while you played quietly on the floor behind me, turning the pages of picture books and reading to yourself in a jabber language only you understand. It was a nice moment that lasted exactly one moment. In the next moment, I glanced behind me and you were gone.

I went from room to room calling your name but there was no answer, which scared me because an absent, quiet toddler is a toddler who has definitely found trouble. Sure enough, I rounded the corner into my bathroom and there you were – standing in front of the toilet holding a half-empty box of Q-tips. You looked up at me and smiled widely, incredibly proud of how you'd just deposited roughly 150 Q-tips into the potty.

I told you firmly that it was a "no-no," which I doubt you'll remember. But I'll certainly remember how I had to find a rubber glove and spend several minutes fishing soggy Q-tips out of the potty. It was a fun morning.

I tell myself this is just a phase – your fascination with the bathroom. About a month ago, your grandma caught you climbing into the potty to use it as a wading pool. Dad caught you sitting in the sink one time, spraying water from floor to ceiling. So this morning's Q-tip debacle convinced me to put child-safety locks on all the bathroom doors. The rest of the day, your big brothers danced wildly outside the door yelling, "Mom, I gotta go. I gotta go! And I can't open the door! HURRY!"

But I don't mind because I'm sure that sprinting up the stairs to open a bathroom door for a panicky 4-year-old is really good cardiovascular exercise for me. Let's face it, I need to be in top physical condition to keep up with you when you're climbing into the dishwasher or repelling down the back of the sofa or running down the driveway to get a closer look at the FedEx truck.

The truth is, Kate, you scare the life out of me nearly every single day. You'd eat a toxic level of Aquafresh toothpaste if I didn't lock it in a high cabinet. You have no reasonable fear of gravity whatsoever. And what you lack in cautious judgment you more than make up for in reckless speed – a very troubling combination in a toddler.

I tell you all this because one day you'll be a teenager, and teenagers are famous for pushing the envelope. But sweetie, you've already done your share of envelope pushing. If you pushed it any more, it would be in an entirely different ZIP code.

Therefore I've decided that you're not allowed do anything reckless during your teen years. I've already paid my dues, you see, and there's only so much a mother's fragile nerves can take.

Having said that, I will tell you that I found a quote from Mark Twain the other day that reminds me of you. He said, "My mother had a great deal of trouble with me, but I think she enjoyed it." And I'm sure she did, just as I'm sure of how much I love you, despite the small heart attack you give me on a regular basis.

Somehow, you balance things out just enough to keep me chugging along. At lunch time today, you pointed to the carton of chocolate milk and said "Peeze?" When I handed you a cup, you said "T'ank eww," which gives me hope that perhaps even little girls made of jalapenos can be civilized.

Sometimes, when I wake you from your nap, your little pink rosebud mouth turns up into the sweetest smile and your eyes flash with excitement for whatever new adventure you've dreamed up next. Your small arms wrap around my neck, and I melt into a pool of maternal love that's far deeper than any trouble you can get into.

Enjoy your teen years, Katie-bug, and try very hard not to make your mother crazy because I'm close enough already. And take it easy on me when you decide you know everything and that I'm holding you back from grown-up adventures. Because even though you may look older, part of my heart and mind will still see you as the 25-pound, 31-inch-tall little girl who tosses Q-tips into the potty.

It will be hard for me to let you go into a world where there are things far more dangerous than eating toothpaste. When I let myself consider it, every instinct I have screams at me to scoop you up, hold you close and rock you safely in my arms until you're 35. I'm pretty sure you wouldn't like that.

But I also know that one day years from now, when you have a baby, you will understand that a mother's instinct to protect is fierce and irrational and, above all else, fueled by a love deeper than you ever thought possible.

So when you're 15 years old and irritated with your old, decrepit mother who is unbearably uncool at times, remember the little rhyme I whisper into your ear at night as you drift off to sleep:

"I loved you yesterday.
I love you still.
I always have.
I always will."

Love,
Mom

Now Entering Barbie Town

Here's an ugly secret mothers try to deny, even to ourselves: Sometimes we buy our daughters a few extra things we probably shouldn't. Is it because we like the girls more? No. We love all our kids equally. Is it because the girls just need more stuff? Maybe sometimes they do, but that's not the reason, either.

It's because deep down, underneath our mature, practical mommy selves, there lives a little girl. And that little girl is wildly attracted to glittery purses, super-soft stuffed animals and precious little outfits with cherries or butterflies on them. Sometimes when we're innocently walking down store aisles, that little girl sneaks out and starts shopping.

I know this because it has happened to me. A few weeks ago, I was pushing 3-year-old Kate around in the shopping cart at Wal-Mart. She was singing the lyrics to "Be Our Guest" for the one-thousandth time. I was heading toward the back of the store, fully intending to walk past the toy aisle without pausing. But then Kate pointed and called out so loudly that it startled me, and I turned to see what had caught her attention. "Beauty!" she said, her eyes wide with excitement. "Mama, it's Belle from Beauty and the Beast!"

I couldn't see exactly what she was talking about, but I was sure she was right because 3-year-old girls can spot a Disney princess from 50 yards away. I knew that, if we didn't turn down that toy aisle, there would be much weeping and gnashing of teeth. So I agreed to push the cart down the aisle so she could get a closer look, but first I issued this warning: "Okay, we'll go see what it is but we're just going to look, okay? Only looking, not getting. You understand?" She nodded her agreement and we turned down the Barbie aisle.

Here's the thing about Barbie. She is, without a doubt, the most cloned woman on the face of the Earth. When I was a girl, there were only a couple of Barbies to collect – a blonde and a brunette. Of course, Ken was there, too, and there was the famous Barbie car. But I could fit my entire Barbie collection into one shoebox.

These days, you'd need a shoebox the size of Texas Stadium to store a complete Barbie collection. Not only has Barbie had 80 different occupations over the years, she also now has pets, furniture and bath-version Barbies whose clothes turn different colors when you dip them in the tub.

And let's not even get started on the clothes. Since her debut, Barbie has had about one billion pieces of clothing and shoes produced for her and her friends.

So I shouldn't have been surprised to discover that Kate's favorite Disney movie has its own Barbie. She wears a beautiful yellow gown, just like her namesake in the movie. I picked her up and handed her to Kate, who noticed that she also comes with a rose-shaped magic wand. The package had a button marked "Try me!" so I did, purely out of curiosity. When I pushed it, the familiar theme song from Beauty and the Beast began to play and then red roses bloomed out from the yellow ball gown. Suddenly my eyes got as wide as Kate's did.

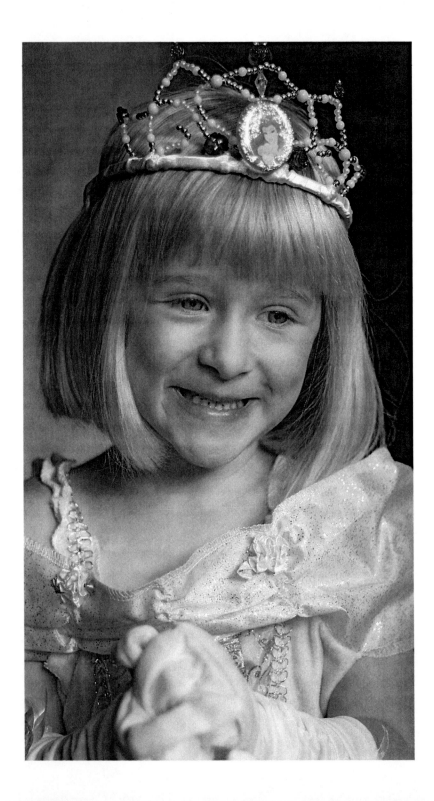

"Oh! Look at the flowers," Kate said. Then, in a tone of awe and reverence, she added softly, "Mama, I love her."

And, as much as I hate to admit it, a little part of me loved her, too. My inner girl was seduced by the combination of nostalgia and new technology. When I was little, Barbie didn't even have a belly button. And now she has roses magically blooming on her ball gown. Will wonders never cease?

I was torn. Inside my head, the Practical Mom side of me sternly said, "We did not come here to get a Barbie. We came here for milk, bread and cereal. Step away from the doll." But it was very hard to hear what Practical Mom was saying because my Inner Girl was a lot louder and more insistent: "She plays music and has a magic wand that makes ROSES BLOOM ON HER DRESS! Are you kidding me? We HAVE to bring her home!"

I stood there for a few moments, as my Inner Girl and Practical Mom duked it out. Wisely, Kate did not plead or beg for the Barbie. She just sat there quietly adoring it, which softened up the Practical Mom just enough for the Inner Girl to win the day.

"Okay, we'll get her, but only this one time," I said firmly. "We are not going to get a Barbie every time we go grocery shopping. You understand?"

And as the words came out of my mouth, I wasn't sure if I was saying them to her or to me. Either way, I hope both of us were listening.

PIRATES, BOOTIE AND OTHER QUESTIONS

As parents, we often find ourselves answering big questions at unusual times. Like during a drive back from the splash park, for example. It was about 96 degrees that day, with a heat index of what felt like 205. "Sweltering" was the word that came to mind.

Eight-year-old Adam asked if we could stop by our favorite ice-cream place on the way home since it was so hot. Normally, I ask the kids to hold their ice cream cups and not eat until we get home, so as not to end up with a car interior coated in chocolate ice cream. But it was too hot that day to wait, so everybody ate while I drove the few miles to our house.

In that short time period, here's the conversation that transpired. Three-year-old Kate kicked it off with this alarming line:

Kate (who was holding her ice cream cup between her legs): "Don't worry, Mom. I'll be careful not to drip the ice cream on my penis."

Me (horrified but trying to sound casual and nonchalant): "What?! No, Kate, girls do not have a penis. That's only for boys. Girls have different parts."

(Side note: Let me interrupt here and say that, years ago, I followed some child-rearing book's advice about not making up cute nicknames for body parts. The book said it's better for kids to know the correct names of the parts of the human body so they won't be confused later on. It made sense at the time. But I'll admit I nearly wrecked the minivan when my 3-year-old girl said the word "penis." A nickname like wee-wee would have been far less jarring. But I digress. I'll pick it up where we left off.)

Jack (6 years old and honestly curious): "If she doesn't have a penis, then where does the pee come out?"

Me (trying to figure out how ice cream could have led to all this): "Well, her part is just different from yours. Pee comes out of her private parts. They're private because nobody should be looking at them or touching them except for Kate. They're private," I said, proud of how I'd delayed the task of trying to teach a 3-year-old how to pronounce the word "urethra."

Jack: "And nobody is supposed to see your naked bootie, right Mom?"

Me: "That's right. Hey, is this ice cream good or what?"

Thankfully, the conversation switched back to the merits of chocolate versus vanilla at that point and I felt relieved. But I also realized that, of all the people in the van, I was the only one who felt awkward about the topic. The kids were just figuring things out and asking questions, as they should. Parents are the ones who bring all the weird baggage to the issue.

When we got home and finished our ice-cream, I told everyone to go upstairs and take baths to wash off the chlorine and sweat. I checked on each of them to make sure soap was being used and armpits scrubbed. Ten minutes later, Kate rounded the corner dressed in her favorite pink Elmo pajamas and sat in front of me while I combed out her wet hair.

"Did you remember to wash your arms and legs and everything else?" I asked.

"Yes," she replied. "And I even remembered to wash my pirate parts."

"Pirate parts?" I asked.

"Yep, the pirate parts, just like you said," she confirmed.

I nodded and switched on the hair dryer, trying not to laugh. Obviously, this won't be our last anatomy lesson.

Pow! Right in the Kisser!

I got a phone call a few weeks ago when 4-year-old Kate was at a gymnastics day camp. The teacher told me there'd been an accident but then quickly added that Kate was okay. I was grateful for the second half of that sentence because my heart jumped into my throat as soon as the word "accident" had been uttered.

During a spirited game of tag, Kate had run head-first into a pole, and her teacher thought she would need to see a doctor or a dentist or both. So I sped toward the gym and raced inside to find her curled up in the lap of a fellow mama, who just happened to be a nurse who was at the gym that day. (As accidents go, it's awfully good to have one when a nice nurse is standing nearby.)

When I knelt down to look at the damage, I saw blood on her shirt and her favorite pink skirt, and her cut lip had already begun to swell to twice its normal size. The gymnastics teacher told me one of her front teeth had been knocked backward and was barely hanging on. I scooped her up in my arms with a plan in mind. Located in a shopping plaza, the gym was only a few steps away from my dentist's office so I rushed her over there and asked if the dentist could see her right away.

Three minutes later, we were in the dentist's chair getting some emergency front-tooth treatment. (One of the top criteria for choosing any doctor, in my opinion, is finding one that will help you out when you're in a parenting panic moment, as I was then.) The dentist numbed Kate's mouth and then went to work trying to save the tooth. Somehow she got it back into place and glued it to the teeth on either side of it, hoping that it would stabilize and tighten back up over the next few weeks.

Her lip didn't need stitches, so we went home with orders to put ice on the swelling, eat only soft foods for several days and watch for any signs that the tooth was turning grey or getting infected. Kate looked pretty rough those first few days – a little like she'd been in a bar fight with those low-life Bratz dolls and had come out on the losing end of it.

A few days later, her lip was getting better and the tooth, although still wobbly, was still there and still white. We cut her favorite foods into small pieces that she could stick in her mouth and chew with her back teeth.

After two weeks of applesauce, yogurt and back-teeth chewing, we went back to the dentist for a follow-up appointment. The news wasn't good. The tooth was still very wobbly and didn't seem to be tightening up as we'd hoped. The dentist did an x-ray that revealed the answer – a fracture through and through near the root of the tooth. In short, it was a goner.

I felt a small sense of loss when the dentist said the tooth had to come out. Sure, it was a baby tooth that was destined to fall out at some point anyway, but I was hoping she could keep that neat little row of baby teeth she always flashes in photos. And I knew that losing a front tooth would immediately make her look older, just as it did when her brothers began to lose their baby teeth. We mom-types tend to get sad when the "baby" of the family starts looking less like a baby.

But it had to be done, so we soldiered through the tooth extraction. Kate was absolutely fearless, only whimpering for a second or two when the numbing injection was given. A few minutes later, it was over. When we left, Kate had a cotton roll sticking out of her mouth and was carrying her baby tooth, which the nurse had encased in a small plastic treasure box. She was very much looking forward to a visit with the Tooth Fairy later that night, and her older brothers told her that losing a tooth was "cool" which definitely earned her some credibility as a big kid.

In the end, I worried for nothing. Because Kate's new snaggle-tooth smile is even more endearing than the one with perfect little teeth. And it matches her personality – headstrong, fearless, quirky and cute. I'll take personality over perfection any day of the week.

Do Things Scared

I got a lesson in bravery today from a 5-year-old girl. Our preschooler, Kate, knew she'd need kindergarten immunizations before she could move into the elementary school big leagues this fall. Her preschool teachers have been talking about it for months now, encouraging everyone in class to submit to kindergarten shots and earn a special toy reward from the "shot box."

The kids who run the kindergarten shot gauntlet also get their names on a poster which proudly displays their achievement. If ever there was a good use of peer pressure, this is it.

After her best friend got her name on the kindergarten shot poster, Kate was in a big hurry to get hers up there, too. I, however, wasn't in a hurry because I've been through kindergarten shots with her two older brothers and remember the drama all too clearly.

But the shots were inevitable so I took advantage of Kate's sense of urgency. Today was the big day.

"You know what's going to happen after you get your kindergarten shots?" I asked as we climbed into the minivan. "We're going to go get the biggest ice cream treat you ever saw in your whole life!"

"The biggest?" she asked, wide-eyed.

"Yep, as big as you want," I confirmed.

This seemed to help, but I could tell she was scared. I distracted her by chatting about ice cream flavors on the way to the clinic, and then we played a game of "I Spy" while we waited for the nurse to come in with the dreaded tray of syringes.

When the moment arrived, I took each of Kate's small hands in mine and told her to squeeze extra hard. I felt her body tense as the first needle went into her upper thigh. Her face flinched harder at the second injection. But the third and last one – that was the biggie. Her face grimaced with the pain, and two tears ran down her cheek.

But then it was over. After applying three Bugs Bunny Band-Aids, the nurse released her and Kate buried her face in my shoulder as I scooped her up and hugged her tight, telling her over and over how well she had done – how brave she'd been. After a few minutes, the relief washed over her and we joyfully walked out of there headed toward the biggest chocolate milkshake of her young life.

The kindergarten shots reminded me of something that's easy to forget when I'm nervous about something. Fear is the thing we all have in common. Just like that classroom full of 5-year-old kids, we're all facing something scary.

We may not be staring down the same monster, but we're all in a stand-off with fear – a job, a scary diagnosis, a loss, a hard conversation, embarrassment, possible failure, what might happen, what might not happen.

I recently heard someone say that sometimes we have to "do things scared." And it struck me as one of the truest things ever said. Kate didn't wait for fear to pass. She didn't wait for self-confidence to wash over her. She walked into the clinic anyway, squeezed my hands, shed a few tears, and came out the other side. She "did it scared," which makes it all the more impressive that she did it at all.

Eleanor Roosevelt once said "You must do the things you think you cannot do." And she was right. But I would add to that bit of wisdom with this: "Do things scared, and then go have ice cream."

ARE WE DONE YET?

Today I slipped on a jacket I hadn't worn in a long time. I walked outside and shivered when I felt how cold the wind was, so I stuck my hands into the pockets. There was something there. I pulled it out and smiled when I saw it – a pink pacifier that used to go everywhere our youngest child went a few years ago. We never left home without it. But now she's nearly 4 years old and has traded in her pacifier for Barbies and hair accessories.

As I held the pacifier in my hand, I wondered what I should do with it. Throw it out? Or stash it in a drawer just in case we need it again. But needing it again would mean there might be another baby in the house someday, which leads me back to a question that has been circling my mind like a diverted plane waiting for a landing strip: "Are we done yet?"

Most days, I'm pretty sure about the answer. Yes, we're done. Three kids equal a house full of joy and chaos and endless things to do. My head knows that we're happy to have finished the baby phase and looking forward to adventures as the kids get older.

But my heart? Well, the heart can't make up its mind. Every now and then I see a woman at the grocery store who's just weeks away from giving birth, and I remember how incredible it was to feel a baby move inside my belly. I remember the anticipation of holding him or her for the first time. I loved the miracle of it all. My head tries to remind my heart that nausea and fatigue and mind-blowing labor pain also came with that package, but the heart is an eternal optimist.

Sometimes I see someone holding a baby who is three or four months old – that wonderful age when babies are snuggly and smiley and thrilled to ride around on your hip just to see the world. And one look at those sweet baby cheeks and pudgy little hands makes my heart start whispering things like "well, maybe…"

Perhaps my ambivalence about it puts me in the minority. Most couples I've talked to know for certain when they're done. In fact, they'll often say it like this: "Oh, we are SO done! Definitely done." But Tom and I have never felt that certain and have therefore sat squarely on the reproductive fence.

I talked to my doctor about all this at my annual check-up last week. I told him that even though I'm 99 percent sure we're done having kids, it makes me sad sometimes to think I'll never again have a newborn fall asleep on my shoulder. His response surprised me.

"Do you have a dog?" he asked.

"What?" I asked.

"I'm talking about a little dog you can cuddle with. My wife got a dog and now she takes it for walks and buys it little sweaters. You need a place for all that mothering energy to go," he said.

"It's funny you should say that because I do have a few friends who recently got little dogs, and they baby those dogs like crazy," I said, remembering how much I loved it when my friend's new terrier curled up in my lap.

"Yep," he said, confirming his diagnosis. "You need a dog."

On the way home, I thought about the concept of a "transitional dog" and how it might help bridge the gap between the baby phase and what lies beyond it. I floated the theory past Tom, who quickly reminded me about the transitional stray cat I'd already brought home a few months earlier. And while our cat Percy is entertaining, in my heart I also know she'd trade my love for a can of tuna any day of the week. Cats are practical that way.

So what's an ambivalent mother to do? Just keep circling the airport until we figure out where to land? My instinct tells me "I'll know when I know" and not to worry too much about it in the meantime. I'll just leave the pink pacifier in my jacket pocket and decide what to do with it later. Until then, maybe I'll buy the cat a little sweater and be glad I won't need to put her through college.

CHAPTER 5

THE SOAPBOX FILE

THE DEMISE OF DECENCY

This will make me sound ancient and utterly un-hip, but here goes: When it comes to fashion, decency is nearly dead. It's just a couple of shorty-shorts away from a total flat-line.

I know fashion is subjective and one person's idea of "sexy" might be another person's idea of "vulgar." And fashion will always try to push boundaries. I grew up seeing Madonna videos on MTV so I get it. What bothers me, both as a woman and a mother, is how often fashion jumps the boundaries altogether and ends up in the ditch.

In the past couple of months, I've taken a few trips that gave me the chance to hit two huge shopping malls. These mega-sized malls not only help you get a pulse on current trends, it's also the perfect place to people-watch. I walked into one store I'd never been in before and quickly realized I was at least a decade too old to be there. The style was definitely aimed at a teenage audience. As I made a U-turn to leave, a pair of shorts caught my eye and I stopped to stare. I picked them up to make sure they were actual shorts because they were so tiny, so barely there, they seemed more like white denim panties fraying along the edges.

I saw at least a handful of girls – most in their teens and early 20s – wearing shorts like that, pairing them with a tank top and platform, dominatrix high heels. And these girls weren't prowling around a nightclub. They were in the mall food court. I saw one at the movie theater for a 7 o'clock show with her date. Every time I spot one, I'm a little stunned because these are the kinds of clothes people used to see only on women working street corners in bad parts of town. Whether they'd ever admit it or not, lots of today's fashion designers are churning out what can only be called "hooker chic."

Before I get called a preachy old prude, let me say that I like clothes that fit. There's nothing wrong with clothes that flatter a woman's figure and make a man's eyes get just a little bit wider when she crosses the room. But there's a line between sexy and skanky. On one side of that line, you're alluring. On the other, you're offensive.

Why haven't women noticed how lopsided this trend is? Boys' and men's clothes aren't all about the size or outline of their various body parts. Men would never go for that. But somehow, women have let fashion designers tell us that tawdry is trendy and smutty is sexy. No matter what label is on it or what celebrity wears it, tawdry and smutty are still exactly that.

What scares me most is what this trend may mean for girls so anxious to wear the "in" thing – as most teenage girls are. A young woman who just wants the end-of-date kiss can end up in a dangerous position if she's with a guy who's convinced – by the booty-grazing shorts and the mostly sheer shirt – that she must want a lot more than that because she has dressed the part.

Assault is never okay for any reason and is certainly never the fault of the woman, no matter how she has dressed. But we'd be kidding ourselves if we let girls grow up believing appearance and presentation could never put you more at risk of violence.

Whether it's an Italian business suit or a skimpy tube top, clothes send messages. People listen.

Parents and women need to use purchasing power to convince the fashion industry that elegance and grace still have a place on the rack and that "hooker chic" is officially out.

THE GOOD FIGHT

I fight this fight over and over again. In one corner sits my constant companion – worry. In the other corner, there is faith. When the bell rings, they approach each other warily, circling, anxious to see who's stronger – who'll win the match. And I feel like a spectator sitting ringside, watching the struggle and sometimes wondering whose side I'm really on.

I've always admitted to being a worrier and often joke that it's in my DNA, as my mother and grandmother were both world-champion worriers as well. If worry was an Olympic sport, we'd have more medals than Michael Phelps.

But when you worry so much that you find yourself worrying about the amount of time you spend worrying, you know you've taken it to a whole new level. And even worse is the realization that perhaps all this worrying collides head-on with the claim that you're a person of faith – which I am. So if I have faith, why can't I stop worrying?

Worrying has always come naturally to me, but it got worse after my brother died 11 years ago. I was newly pregnant with my first child when it happened, and the sudden loss of someone so close made the already tenuous pregnancy that much more complicated and scary. A few weeks after the funeral, Tom insisted I go see a grief counselor. We didn't know it at the time, but the counselor also happened to be a trained nurse who had worked for years on the maternity floor of a hospital.

Her name was Pan, and she helped me through the hardest year of my life. And she taught me a lot about worry. One day in her office, I mentioned something that was really worrying me. I can't remember what I said I was worried about, but I'll never forget her reply: "Haven't you figured out yet that you're not God? Do you realize you're not in control of everything?"

The look on my face must have told her how horrified and embarrassed I was that she thought I could ever think of myself in those terms. I stammered around trying to explain myself and then she put her hand on mine and said softly, "It's okay. I understand. You're just worried that God isn't always on the job, and that maybe he wasn't on the job when your brother died."

Upon hearing those words, fresh tears stung my eyes because I knew she was right. I was having such a hard time imagining how God could let it happen. Deep down, in a part of myself I would have never admitted to, I thought something disastrous might happen again if God went on coffee break or stepped away to help somebody else.

So I worried. And on some level, maybe I used the worry as a superstitious immunization against catastrophe. If I worried about something enough, maybe it wouldn't ever happen. My big worry monster would scare it off before it had a chance to knock the wind out of me.

If this were a perfect world, this paragraph would be the spot where I describe how I finally conquered my worrying problem and how I now skip merrily down the street and never lie awake at night. But it's not. I'm still neurotic. Writing is good therapy for people like me because it lets us sort out our mental stuff on paper and try to make peace with it.

I've accepted that worry is a part of who I am. Everyone has something they grapple with. Some people are diabetic, and some people are anxious. I'm anxious – probably always will be. I can work around it for the most part as long as I remind myself that, even when things don't go according to plan, they are still – somehow – part of God's plan. And no matter what, the plan is good.

In that mental boxing ring, where worry and faith are locked in battle, I won't lie and say the good guy always wins. But I'm rooting for faith, and I believe it's stronger. And despite my worrisome nature, I can fight the good fight.

A Nice Visit

I had a nice visit the other day.

It was a few weeks before Christmas and I was in a crowded mall having soup and salad in the food court, trying to find the determination to elbow my way through throngs of busy shoppers.

An older man approached the table where I sat alone. He asked if he could sit at the other end, two chairs away on the opposite side. I said sure. He wasn't eating. He was just carrying a shopping bag and looking for a place to rest.

I went on eating my soup. A teenage mall worker came over and wiped down our table. The old man said "hello" to her and remarked about how busy they were that day. She gave a half-smile and nodded her head. He said he hoped she didn't have to work too hard. She ducked her head and went to the next table with her cleaning rag.

A few more minutes passed, and then he caught my eye and asked me a question:

"Are you doing your Christmas shopping today?"

I told him I was trying to get started. Then I returned to my soup, as if it needed my full attention. He spoke up again: "Do you go to my church? I think I've seen you before."

I said "no," it wasn't me. He asked where I go to church and I told him.

"That's good," he said, apparently glad I was a churchgoer, no matter what steeple I was under.

He was a sweet, gentle-looking man with a slight frame, white hair and large glasses. Wearing a plaid red shirt and a gray jacket, he kept his hands folded across his shopping bag. Perhaps his harmless appearance is what made me comfortable enough to return the small talk.

I asked if he was doing his Christmas shopping, and he told me he was there with his daughter – that he'd given her $20 to go pick something out for his son-in-law while he rested. That led to more talk, like the fact that he has three daughters and some grandchildren. He was glad to have a big family.

Somehow through our meandering conversation, I also learned that he'd been through three operations in the past two years and some physical therapy. He'd been in a car accident two years earlier – an accident that took the life of his wife.

"Things were a lot different then," he said. "I was 80 years old and we were both in good health. We drove everywhere and did everything together."

But now he doesn't drive anymore. He misses his wife. She would have loved Christmas with all the family, he said.

He said all these things with the same smile he sat down with at my table. There was a hint of sadness but mostly, there was calm acceptance.

"I turned it over to the Lord," he said. "I figure he knows best and I don't. But I do believe I'll see her again someday." And with that statement, his face lit up a little more, with the anticipation of that future reunion.

Meanwhile, I was trying to swallow the basketball-sized lump in my throat. I nodded my head and listened closely. In the hustle and bustle of the mall, I'd come face to face with an illustration of love and simple kindness. He was the kind of person who had faith in the hardest of times. The kind who holds on to joy. Meeting him was a blessing – the kind that warms you up from the inside out.

We'd been chatting at least five minutes when he asked my name. But it was noisy in the mall so I didn't understand the question right away. I leaned toward him, straining to hear.

He took my hesitation as reluctance and quickly added, "You don't have to tell me if you don't want to."

But I did want to, so I told him my name. Then he told me his – it was Virgil. About that time, another older man approached our table and called his name. It was time to go. He gathered his bag and rose slowly from the table toward his friend. He looked back at me and smiled and said, "It sure was nice to visit with you."

I answered, "It sure was."

I thought about Virgil long after our visit ended because I learned something about myself that day. The truth was that, when he sat down at my table, I was secretly hoping he wouldn't talk to me. Like so many of us, I've become used to protecting my "personal space." You never know about people these days. And I was in a hurry – no time for niceties with strangers in the mall.

But Virgil visited anyway, perhaps because that's what his generation does. They were raised believing that it's right to be friendly to people, all people, even the ones cleaning tables or sitting two chairs away in a crowded food court. They were taught that you should look a person in the eye. And it was common practice to share your name.

Virgil's visit made me realize that maybe my generation has lost something valuable. Maybe we're so uneasy about the steady stream of reports about weirdos and stranger danger that we're now much more comfortable keeping our heads down rather than exchanging a simple kindness with people around us.

Like that teenage mall worker wiping down tables, we're genuinely taken aback when someone speaks kindly to us. It's easier to grunt a half-response and walk away rather than trust someone enough to connect with them, even for a moment.

But I'm grateful Virgil asked to sit at my table. That simple visit made a crowded mall feel a lot more human. And I smiled at strangers the rest of the day and even said hello a few times. Because I want to be more like Virgil.

I want to re-learn the art of having "a nice visit."

Waiting in Line

They say life is a series of moments and most slip by unnoticed. Last night, I witnessed a moment – a big one – and I haven't stopped thinking about it.

It was Sunday night, and I reluctantly made a trip to Wal-Mart to replenish a dangerously low diaper supply. It was a rainy, cool evening and the store was crowded. After a half-hour of shopping, I pushed my cart to the front and surveyed the length of each checkout lane. They all looked about the same, so I picked one and used the first few minutes of the wait to read magazine headlines.

The line slowly inched close enough for me to begin loading my groceries onto the conveyor belt. As I stacked packages of diapers and wipes onto the counter, I noticed that the person ahead of me only had two items. I was mentally congratulating myself for picking the shortest line when I took a second look and realized what those two items were – an EPT home pregnancy test and a package of Skittles.

The combination of the two items struck me as odd, and I glanced up to see who was standing next to them. And there they were – two teenage girls, who looked no older than 16, with a very quiet mission: Get the test and get out of there.

One of the girls was buying the test, and the other looked to be her friend, along to lend courage and support. Perhaps they threw in the package of Skittles to make buying the test seem less conspicuous. But the candy only underscored the fact that she was still herself a child, trying to find out whether or not she would soon be having one.

The two girls didn't talk while they stood there. They just waited and tried to look casual, but they must have been scared. And I felt scared for them. When I had first glimpsed the pregnancy test, I remembered the joy I felt when my own test sticks turned positive – the first time I knew my babies were on the way.

But that was an entirely different scene than the one in front of me. More than a decade of maturity, experience and education separated me from the girl in front of me, just like the bar dividing her pregnancy test from my jumble of groceries and diapers.

Knowing what I know now – that parenthood is the most ambitious, overwhelming job a person ever has – I can't imagine doing it without the emotional and financial resources you need just to get by.

I glanced at the girl's ring finger to confirm my assumptions about her age. On that finger was a large senior class ring that likely belongs to a boy who will also be impacted by the result of the test.

The mothering part of me wanted to tap the girl on the shoulder and tell her everything would be okay. That no matter what the result, she would find a way through it. Instead, I said nothing – partly because it's not polite to intrude in someone's private life while waiting in line at Wal-Mart and partly because I just didn't know if everything really would be okay.

The line kept moving and eventually the girls, along with their Skittles and pregnancy test, disappeared through the sliding doors and into the night. Somewhere across town in somebody's bathroom, the girls would wait on another line to appear or not appear. Would this be a moment that would change the course of her life, or would it be a moment she looks back on as a scary close call?

There's no way to know what the result was, but I can't help thinking about that nervous girl, the boy who gave her his class ring, and the baby – who may or may not be part of their future. I can only pray that they make it – all three of them – one way or another.

THE BRIDGE LESS TRAVELED

Not far from my house is a little bridge. I should say "was" a little bridge. It's not there anymore.

But only a few weeks ago, I used to cross it every day on my way to and from work. It was a narrow, one-lane bridge with a little white sign on either end that read "3 cars at a time." It was in a tiny town sandwiched between two larger cities.

Traffic would stop at the bridge and, depending on which car got there first, one lane of traffic would cross over, three cars at a time. Once the way was clear, three more cars from the other direction would cross.

People coming off the bridge would nod or wave at the people waiting on the other end, as if to say, "Thank you, now it's your turn." It would continue this way, all day and into the night. Nodding, waving, taking turns – the kind of courtesy that's common in the country.

But during the busiest times of day, the road got backed up while cars waited for each lane to trickle across. Often I'd sit there waiting impatiently, irritated that the bridge wasn't big enough for two-way traffic. Didn't they realize we're all in a hurry? Why didn't they fix it already?

Then one day, they did.

Bulldozers and men in orange vests showed up and started building a new bridge right beside the tiny one. They worked for months, while traffic continued trickling across the original bridge. I was glad to see the progress. Soon there'd be no reason to stop and wait.

Finally the new bridge opened for two-way traffic and the old bridge was barricaded. Then they dismantled it piece by piece so they could make the new bridge even wider. You can hardly tell the old one ever existed.

Then the men in orange took their traffic cones and disappeared as suddenly as they'd come, leaving behind a road and a bridge that's straighter, wider and faster. The black asphalt stretches out long and smooth, broken only by bright yellow lines.

It does, however, look a little out of place in the tiny town. The bridge covers more square footage than the town's post office or gas station. It's nothing like the rest of the curvy streets shaded by old oak trees.

But it's much faster. Not two but four lanes whiz past one another without even slowing down. And there's no gathering of people waiting on either end of the bridge anymore.

But there's also no more waving. No friendly nods. No taking turns. There's not an extra second to stop and notice what's blooming at the garden nursery nestled by the roadside. At 35 mph, it's just a green blur.

And it's funny because now I can't even remember why I was in such a hurry to get across the little bridge. What was I rushing to? The new bridge is too fast for waves and nods and somehow I feel the poorer for it.

The one-lane country bridge slipped into the future, into progress. And I suppose it's for the best. Better roads. Safer, perhaps. Better infrastructure is better for business, better for tourism, better for getting to and from work.

But I can't help missing the old bridge for the way it joined two stretches of road and, at the same time, connected us to each other with something as simple as a wave or a nod. It afforded us small, extra moments of time – a precious commodity in an awfully fast lifetime. It made us slow down, take turns and take notice.

And I thought it was just a bridge.

But Wait, There's More

About an hour ago, something happened that made me realize we've had far too much TV time during the long holiday break from school. I came downstairs to make lunch and found 8-year-old Adam sitting at the counter watching the small kitchen television.

"Mom, you need one of those SunSetters," he said.

"What's a SunSetter, and why do I need one?" I asked.

"You know, it's a thing that protects you from harmful UV rays and, if you order now, you'll get $200 off! You just can't find a better value anywhere," he said, sounding much more like an infomercial than a little boy.

"I think we're getting by just fine without a SunSetter. Let's turn off the television for a while," I said.

Thankfully, this particular commercial for motorized awnings was pretty harmless. But there are so many ads with phrases I don't want my kids repeating. With television shows, there's a programming schedule so you know when to avoid the cartoons and shows you don't want your kids to see. Parents can even block entire channels.

With commercials, it's a surprise attack. By the time you realize what the ad is for and try to change the channel, you're already 15 seconds into it, which is just long enough for your kids to start asking what Trojans are. The ads pop up like a bad rash at the most inopportune times. (Ironically, some of the commercials are, in fact, about bad rashes. But I digress.)

Can't the technology gurus come up with a warning system so parents have a fighting chance? A loud beep, maybe, to let us know something questionable is on the way? Raising kids is tough enough without having a toddler sing the theme song "Viva Viagra" during a visit from grandparents.

And who needs Viagra anyway? If the commercials from Victoria's Secret don't get a guy going, then I'm betting nothing will. My boys aren't nearly old enough to meet Victoria and her model friends, so I wish they'd stop heaving their D-cup "secrets" all over our TV.

When I was a kid, the most embarrassing thing on television involved someone pouring blue liquid on maxi-pads to illustrate how absorbent they were. Every now and then, a Summer's Eve commercial would come on and some poor lady would mention her "not-so-fresh" feeling, but that's about as graphic as it got.

There are a lot more land mines on television today, and it's getting tougher and tougher to dodge them. There are certain discussions the kids and I just aren't ready for yet. I don't want to explain why the man and woman in the KY personal lubricant commercials look so happy.

I don't want to tell them what a "Plan B" over-the-counter pill might do. And we sure don't want to tell them that some people actually take "male enhancement vitamins." Can't we just let them be kids who aren't burdened with too much adult information?

It's not that I'm anti-advertising. I love clever, funny commercials and worked on several of them at an ad agency during my pre-kids career. I just wish that, at least during the day and early evening hours, we could see ads for things like Cheerios and Band-Aids and Tide and Welch's grape jelly – things that kids can more easily wrap their minds around.

We all know childhoods aren't nearly as innocent as they once were. But kids are growing up soon enough without having the world push them along faster in 30-second doses.

A DOSE OF REALITY

I read an article this week that made me rethink a secret I've kept for 10 years. My closest friends know but it's not something I've ever written about – for a lot of reasons. Ten years ago I wrote a column about the devastating loss of my big brother, my only sibling, who died in his sleep at the age of 34.

What I didn't say in that column was that he died after taking too much prescription medication. I didn't say it because I didn't want people to assume it was a suicide – which it wasn't. He was a happy guy with a new job, lots of friends and plans for the future. And I didn't say it because I didn't want people to make the wrong assumptions about what kind of person he was or what kind of upbringing we had. When an "addict" dies, people often see it as less tragic because the person who died bore some of the fault.

I knew people would make negative assumptions because that's what I used to do. When I heard the word "addict," my mind immediately thought of a bum on the street shooting heroin and robbing gas stations. But the truth is that addicts can be very normal. My brother was. He had a good job, friends, values, faith in God, generosity and a sense of humor that absolutely lit up the room.

His problem with prescription painkillers started after a back injury in his late 20s. When the back pain went away, the pills didn't. Like so many of us, he underestimated just how highly addictive pills like these really are. I think he thought, because it was medicine, it was somehow safe – that he could control it.

On the night of April 19, 2001, my brother went to bed and likely took one dose too many of the painkiller hydrocodone along with a common sleeping medication. He had always struggled with insomnia and knew the medicine would help him get to sleep so he could get up for work the next morning. But he didn't get up. Sometime during that night, his lungs just – stopped. And when they did, so did life as we knew it.

What I now know, after reading a government report released this week, is that this kind of story is becoming more common. Deaths from prescription overdoses have tripled in the past 10 years alone. In 1999, there were about 4,000 narcotic deaths. In 2008 – the same year actor Heath Ledger died in his sleep from an accidental overdose – there were more than 15,000 deaths. The rate has tripled, which means it's not just my family's sad story. It's the whole country's story. One U.S. health official called it "an epidemic."

One of the scariest parts of this story is that I can't point to any one thing that caused my brother to start taking more pills. When someone you love dies, you want so badly for it to make sense – to figure out why and how it all went so wrong so maybe you can prevent it from ever happening again. And I've analyzed it a million different ways during the past 10 years and I still can't figure out exactly how we might have stopped it.

One of the biggest problems was that, in my brother's mind, it wasn't a problem. Prescription painkiller addiction is a subtle, insidious thing. It's the slippery slope that takes you down before you even realize you're falling.

I'm finally letting go of the family secret because perhaps one of the best things I can do, especially knowing that the death rate has tripled, is to point to the statistics and to my own story and hope that – for someone reading this – it might be a life-saving dose of reality.

CHAPTER 6

THE PETS & PESTS
FILE

A Fish Story

Every summer my mother packed my bag and dropped me off on my grandparents' farm with a week's worth of miniature cereal boxes and a can of bug spray.

I was 7 years old on the first trip, and, on my second day there, Grandpa said we were going fishing because I'd never been. So he packed up our poles while Grandma tied an oversized sun hat on my head. We picked up Grandma's sister, Aunt Eunice, and the four of us rode down a dusty road with a little green fishing boat trailing behind the truck.

Once we were in the boat trolling along the banks, Grandpa opened the tackle box. They all began rigging their lines with colorful plastic worms, discussing which ones were likely to get a bite. Grandpa tied a red plastic bobber on my line and told me to watch it closely because when it dipped under water, it was time to pull up the fish.

I fished hard during the first hour, never taking my eyes off the bobber. But after a while, I got frustrated. Grandpa had already hauled in three fish and I worried that he'd catch every fish in the lake before they had a chance to swim by my line. He'd just caught his fourth fish when I asked Grandma how he was able to catch so many while I was still waiting for my first.

She nudged the brim of her sun hat up and glanced at Grandpa and then at me. "I don't know, honey. I guess he's holding his mouth just right."

Not knowing that old country sayings run rampant in a fishing boat, I took her at her word. I spent the next hour studying Grandpa's face, mirroring the exact position of his mouth, which was stern and straight except for the occasional sip of Pepsi. I held my mouth just the same way, waiting for the bobber to suddenly dive beneath the murky water.

But the tug never came and soon the sun drained my energy. Aunt Eunice took my pole and propped it in the handle of the ice-chest with the line still in the water, promising to keep an eye on it for me. Grandma made a bed of life vests in the floor of the boat, and I settled down for a nap.

I don't know how long I'd been sleeping when Aunt Eunice started yelling. "You've got a fish! You've got a fish!"

I sat up, rubbing my eyes, and saw that the bobber had disappeared and the fishing line was taut and quivering with the weight of the fish below.

Grandma grabbed the little pole and yanked it up. Out of the water sprang a shimmering gray-green fish, flailing against the hook. She handed me the pole and told me to keep the dangling fish out of the water while Grandpa got the net. Once it was hauled in, Grandpa unhooked it and held it up so I could get a good look at my catch. "That's a fine fish," he said, dropping it into the catch bucket.

Aunt Eunice said, "See there? You caught your first fish!" And Grandma and Grandpa agreed, saying over and over what a fine fish it was. I desperately wanted to take credit for the catch but there was no denying I'd been asleep when it happened. And it's hard to feel proud when you've been out-fished by an ice-chest full of Pepsi.

Nevertheless, it had been an exciting day. With plenty of fish in the bucket, we headed for home and a country supper of fried fish and potatoes. At the end of the week, when the tiny cereal boxes and the bug spray ran out, my mother came back for me. She asked what fun things we'd done, and I told her we'd gone fishing.

"Did you catch anything?" she asked, and I struggled for an answer. Grandma stepped in, "She's so good, she can catch 'em with her eyes closed." And I agreed. It was the truest fish story I'd ever heard.

House Gone Wild

There's a mouse in our house. I saw a brief flash of him last week as he sprinted across the fireplace hearth. I jumped onto the back of the sofa, squealing like a tween at a Jonas Brothers concert, and watched anxiously as Tom set traps to catch him.

Fast forward two days later. Four-year-old Jack bounded upstairs mid-afternoon and raced into my home office, wide-eyed and out of breath.

"Mom! I need you!" he said.

"What's wrong? What is it?" I asked, scanning him for blood or bruises.

"I saw it in the hallway. A chipmunk!"

Normally, I would dismiss this kind of claim and go right ahead with my work. I don't want to say all 4-year-olds are liars, but I will say this: If I had a dollar for every monster a four year old saw, I'd be counting my money on a beach in Aruba right now. But this time the emotion behind the tall tale seemed genuine, so I asked a few more questions.

"Where did you see this chipmunk?" I asked.

"In the hallway downstairs, by the door. Come on, I'll show you," he said, insistent on leading me to the scene of the chipmunk spotting.

"It ran out right here, and then it went down there and it was very fast," he said, re-enacting the chipmunk's path.

"So then what happened? Where did it go?" I asked, expecting that this was the point where his unlikely story would fall apart.

"I opened the door and it went outside," he said.

"Seriously? You opened the door and it ran outside?" I asked. He nodded his head solemnly and never once flashed his tell-tale smirk that indicates he's lying.

Over the next few hours, I grilled Jack about the chipmunk encounter, expecting that the story would change with each telling. It didn't. He was certain about every detail, so I probed further.

"What did this chipmunk look like?" I asked in my best detective voice.

"He had red eyes!" Jack said.

I flashed back two days prior to the mouse-spotting. I asked one more question that was sure to cinch it, one way or another.

"Jack, what did the chipmunk's tail look like?" I asked.

"His tail was kinda long and skinny," he said.

I knew then that Jack's chipmunk was my mouse. And I really hope the part of the story about Jack letting the "chipmunk" out of the house is true because our mouse traps are still empty. I can just imagine my neighbors sipping coffee and watching out the window as our preschooler played doorman for vermin.

Fast forward to the end of the week. I'd just arrived home from driving carpool and realized the garage door was locked. Tom's car was in the driveway, so I walked around to the front door. As I rounded the corner, I saw our sprinkler repair guy standing on the front steps, waiting for Tom to answer the door.

"Hi," I said. "Are you waiting for Tom?"

"Yes," he said and then pointed his finger toward a potted plant by the door. "Is that a real snake sitting there?"

"SNAKE!" I yelled, and then I'm pretty sure I levitated off the ground a foot or so and backed up several feet.

There it was, a black and green snake curled up on the edge of a large potted plant nestled into a bed of ivy. He was perfectly still, which made the sprinkler guy think it might be fake. (For the record, anyone who would have a fake snake greeting people by the front door is not someone I'd want to know.)

I sent Tom out on a murderous mission to kill the snake, but the vile thing made a quick escape. (I didn't care whether or not it was a so-called harmless garden snake. In my book, any snake capable of triggering a heart attack is not a "harmless" snake. He's got to go. Period.)

I suppose we've been lucky in that, after nearly four years of living in a house that backs up to the woods, this is the first snake encounter we've had. He probably showed up on our steps last week because he heard Jack was letting mice out the front door. Just a guess.

The good news is that — other than the few years the mouse and snake sighting shaved off my life — nobody got hurt. The bad news is that there is still a mouse, a snake and quite possibly a chipmunk on the loose around here. And I'm nervous. Very, very nervous.

Shave and a Haircut

Sometimes, in an effort to save money, we take on things we have no business messing around with – things best left to trained professionals. We put on our practical "do it yourself" hats and say stupid, fate-tempting things like "How hard could it be?" And then we find out.

When temperatures hit 90 degrees last week, I told Tom we'd have to make an appointment to get our dogs, Holly and E.J., shaved for the summer, as we do every year around this time. He agreed, hesitantly, because he knew the trip to the doggie salon for two large dogs usually runs around $150.

But there was no question it needed to be done, especially for Holly, who has more fur than your average polar bear. Thirteen years ago, we adopted her as a puppy from a local shelter. All we knew about her was that she was a sweet, tiny, blonde ball of soft fur. The people at the shelter told us she was a Newfoundland breed, and we smiled and said that sounded nice because, at the time, we had no idea that Newfoundland puppies grow up to be roughly the size of a Volkswagen.

When I took her to the veterinarian for shots, I stroked her soft fur and explained to the vet that she was a Newfoundland puppy we'd just adopted. An older man who'd seen his share of puppies, the vet chuckled and told me I didn't adopt a Newfoundland dog. "Well, then what kind of dog is she?" I asked.

"A little yellow dog," he replied, making it clear she was simply a mixed breed true to her pound-puppy heritage.

As our little yellow dog grew up, we were relieved that she didn't get enormous. The vet was right about her mixed breed status, but I believe she must have a Newfoundland somewhere in her gene pool because her fur is impossibly thick and starts shooting out of her skin in huge tufts of wispy hair about this time of year. If we didn't shave her in this heat and humidity, she'd probably self-combust.

So Tom decided to solve two problems with one trip to Wal-Mart. He came home with a $40 set of electric dog clippers, which he said would allow us to shave the dogs and keep more than $100 in our pocket. Brilliant plan, right?

The electric clippers came with an instructional video on how to trim your dog's hair. We watched the first five minutes of the video but then turned it off because the script sounded like it had been written for idiots. It talked about how the "proper use of this excellent grooming tool could even improve our dog's self-esteem." Jeesh! We didn't have time to hear about dog psychology. We were ready to get the job done.

So we set up lawn chairs in the garage and brought in Holly, assuring her it wouldn't hurt a bit. And we didn't physically hurt her during the hour-long shaving debacle, but, if the poor thing sees her reflection in a rain puddle anytime soon, her self-esteem will go right into the toilet. She looks – how should I say it – rough. Real rough. It turns out that shaving a dog is not nearly as easy as it looks on the instructional video.

On the bright side, there are a few areas of her hair I'm proud of – smooth, wide swaths of short hair that look almost like a professional's work. The problem is that those few smooth spots are surrounded by clumps and lumps we couldn't quite get to as well as naked divots where we were a tad too aggressive with the clippers. In short, she looks like she was shaved by a hay thrasher. A frustrated, misguided hay thrasher who did not watch the instructional video.

We didn't finish the haircut completely. After more than an hour of shaving, we knew Holly was tired of our amateur grooming efforts and we were exhausted and covered in enough dog hair to create an additional dog. The dog's legs were still kind of shaggy but we'd managed to get the bulky hair off her body.

Before the haircut, she weighed about 70 pounds. She must be considerably lighter now, though, since it seems like we shaved off at least 15 pounds of hair – most of which is still rolling around the floor of our garage like Texas tumbleweeds.

We were too tired to tackle shaving the second dog that same weekend, so we're putting it off until next Saturday. But after the second dog sees the job we did on the first, there's a good chance he might run away before the weekend. Who could blame him? I hope he gets a professional haircut before he comes back home.

Something Squirrely

When you live next to a wooded lot, you also live next to critters. Over the years we've seen deer, chipmunks, mice, armadillos, woodpeckers, rabbits and even a couple of snakes. Other than the anxiety the snake sightings caused, we haven't had much trouble from the wild neighbors.

But last week some neighborhood squirrels set up housekeeping inside a wall of our garage. Tom listened to the bumping, scratching sound and followed it to the wall between the kitchen and garage. The next morning, he even saw the furry squatter scamper outside when he opened the garage door.

I don't hate squirrels, but I don't want one of them running across my foot as I haul groceries from the van to the house. And listening to squirrels run laps in the kitchen wall was unsettling. The squirrels had to go.

I typed "how to catch a squirrel" into Google's search engine and found out we weren't the only ones dealing with uninvited squirrels. The advice on how to evict them ranged from large rat traps and poisoning – which seemed too extreme – to putting some bait into a "live catch" cage and waiting for the squirrel's appetite to do the rest.

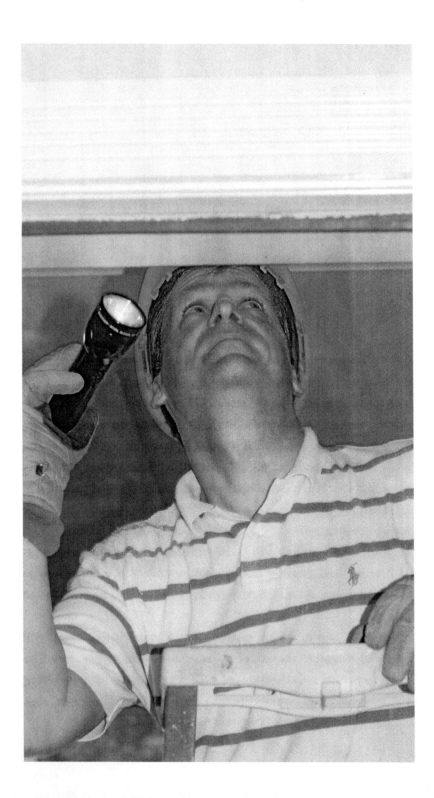

We decided to go the more humane route. Tom went to the store and came back with a live-catch trap. But first he wanted to find out how the squirrel was getting into the wall. There were no obvious points of squirrel entry, so, as men will often do, he cut a big hole into the wall to get a better look. Then he stuck his head in and looked around but still found no opening large enough for a squirrel (although he'd just cut a rather large squirrel opening into the wall, which I politely did not point out.)

Meanwhile, the squirrel wasn't falling for the live-catch trap in the garage. After finding the cage empty for a week, Tom decided he should put the trap into the ceiling space where he could hear the pitter-patter of squirrel feet. But first he'd need to cut another large hole into the ceiling so he could fit the trap up there.

Obviously, I wasn't pleased about the squirrels or the holes, but it was out of my hands. A smart woman knows when a man is on a mission and does not interfere with that mission, even when the garage is beginning to look like Swiss cheese. It was man versus squirrel, and a man cannot let a bushy-tailed opponent invade his castle. This was his own suburban version of Caddyshack.

After two weeks, two holes and lots of banging around on the walls with a broom handle, Tom snapped. Wearing an orange hard hat, a pair of goggles and heavy gloves, he put a ladder below the hole he'd cut in the ceiling and told me to stand next to it.

"What am I supposed to be doing here?" I asked, thinking he had a plan in place.

"Just stand there so you'll be able to tell the ER doctor what happened to me in case this doesn't go well," he said.

He climbed the ladder and his head and shoulders disappeared into the hole.

"There are three of them up here!" he said. "They're burrowing into the ceiling insulation. I'm going in after them!"

Then there was a loud yell – from Tom, although I'm sure the squirrels were probably screaming, too – and then a squirrel jumped down out of the hole, onto Tom's shoulder, off his back and onto the ground where he sprinted out of the garage. We didn't see where the other two squirrels went, but we're hoping they let themselves out of whatever hole they'd come in through. Tom said that, when he reached for the squirrel, all he saw was his furry nemesis flying straight toward his face.

He doused the squirrel's hideout with a black pepper spray that's supposed to discourage them from hanging around, and then he climbed back down the ladder sneezing like crazy. Score one for the man, zero for the varmints.

Fortunately, we haven't heard or seen the squirrels return to the walls and ceiling. They're probably up a tree somewhere telling tales of the monster in the orange hat with wide eyes and big hands that came after them that fateful day. My guess is they'll keep a safe distance for a while – or at least until we get those two big holes patched.

A Tough Decision

Today Tom and I faced the moment we've both dreaded for weeks now. We took our sweet blonde dog, Holly, to the vet's office, and we came home without her. She was 14 – or 98 in dog years – and she was like sunshine in a dog's body. Part of me desperately wanted the vet to talk us out of it, to say there was something else we could try that would give her back the quality of life she deserved. But she didn't. She said it was time, that she would make the same decision if it were her own dog.

Still, the reassurance didn't make it any less gut-wrenching as I sat next to her on the floor, holding her head in my lap as she licked Tom's hand for the last time and we told her over and over again that she was a good girl. Right now I am equal parts devastated by what we have done and certain it was the right thing to do.

So today I'm remembering something I wrote four years ago on a happier day, in hopes it'll make you smile and remind you to hug your dog.

Four years earlier…

This morning I looked out the kitchen window and saw our dogs, Holly and E.J., lying on the deck in a patch of sunlight. Sprawled out

143

alongside each other, the curve of their backs fit together like puzzle pieces. I tapped on the glass, and their sleepy heads jerked up as I opened the window. They scrambled toward me, knowing that if the kitchen window opened then surely a leftover was about to come flying out. I tossed them the leftover crusts of toast one of the kids left behind at breakfast.

Holly jumped up to catch the airborne bread, landing with a thud and a grunt. E.J. let his piece bounce off his nose and then shuffled toward it, wondering if a dry piece of toast was really worth this much effort. Watching them move slowly and stiffly in the cool morning air made me silently admit something no dog lover wants to think about. They're getting older, slower, greyer. And no matter how much or how well we love them, dogs don't live forever.

I walked outside to give them a long overdue scratch behind the ears. They welcomed me warmly and seemed to hold no grudge that I hadn't had as much time for visits these past few years while I've been busy raising babies. They bumped against my legs, licked my hands and fidgeted excitedly at the sound of my voice.

In dog years, Holly and E.J. are in their 70s – not ancient by any means but they definitely qualify for the senior citizen discount. A stray and a shelter adoptee, they're both the most popular breed of dog there is, which is part Labrador, part who-knows. What they lack in pedigree they make up for in personality.

I stroked the thick golden hair on Holly's back and came away holding a few tufts of it that seem to shed every time I touch her. She smiled her wide, toothy smile and wriggled into me, asking for more. Despite her age, she still has a puppy's heart. Eleven years ago, just days after adopting her, we watched her sprint playfully around our living room. Then she would suddenly fall to the floor, close her eyes and her plump little body would rapidly heave up and down while she caught her breath.

After a minute or two on the floor, she'd pop back up and continue her romp as if nothing had happened. Five minutes later, she'd collapse again. We were afraid she had a seizure disorder, but she was fine. She just loved playing so much that she'd do it until she literally dropped.

Eager for his turn, E.J. scooched Holly aside. He put his black head in my hands, and I brought my nose to his. I noticed all the silver hairs that have begun to frame his eyes, making him look like a distinguished

EJ

HOLLY

old man. It's a nice addition because E.J. has always been what I call "cosmetically challenged." A stray found roaming on a golf course, E.J. had what must have been a terrible puppyhood. When we brought him home, he had only one ear (hence the name Earless Joe, or E.J. for short.) The other ear had been cruelly cut off by someone who will one day have a special spot in Hell, if you ask me. The skin around his eyes was damaged, and, for the first six months we knew him, his tail stayed tucked firmly between his legs. With time and love, his tail found the courage to rise and eventually even wag.

But he still battles the demons of his past. When a repairman came to the house last week, E.J. glued himself to my legs and hid his scarred face behind my knees. I could feel him trembling, as this unfamiliar man stirred up memories of past abuse. Even in his old age, E.J. is still shy, vulnerable and afraid. And I indulge him because he deserves a mama who will protect him.

I felt guilty sitting there with the dogs, knowing I owe them an apology. I swore nothing would change when we had kids and that the dogs would get just as much attention as before. But the past six years have seen the addition of one, two and now three kids in the house. And with each child, the dogs have accepted a number of downgrades – from sleeping in our bed to sleeping on an old blanket in the garage, from special doggie treats to scraps of toast and chicken nuggets the kids didn't eat. And time – well, there's just never enough of it. Yet they love us as much as they ever did – even more.

So I gave them an extra belly rub and they trotted off to intimidate squirrels and patrol the yard's perimeter. And I went inside, hoping they'll continue to be blessed with good health so we can continue to be blessed by them.

ASKING FOR THE SALE

When we left last weekend for our little cabin in the woods, we had five family members in the minivan. When we returned, there were six. Here's how it happened:

On Saturday a small gray cat showed up to greet us at the cabin. She weaved between our legs and opened her mouth to "meow," although no sound came out. We weren't surprised to see her because the cabin is on one of those woodsy roads where pets wander from house to house. Our kids sometimes play with two of the neighbor's dogs who trot down the street when we've got burgers cooking on the grill.

But this cat stuck around for hours, sleeping on the deck and rushing to the door any time someone came out. The kids wanted to pet her, so I checked her out to make sure she was friendly. When we started petting, I realized this was probably not a pet that was out for a Saturday stroll. Underneath her long gray hair, I felt nothing but bones. She was starving, and her mute "meow" couldn't even tell us how bad it was.

We cut up some bologna and cheese and fed her, although Tom (who has always been "anti-cat") insisted we do it a few yards from the

147

house so she wouldn't think of our place as "home." She gobbled down the food quickly.

After the kids went to bed, Tom and I sat in the living room reading and watching TV. About 9 p.m., a little gray head with pointy ears appeared in the window closest to where Tom was sitting. She put one paw up on the window and mouthed her silent "meow" while staring deep into Tom's eyes.

"Look who's here," Tom said warily, nodding toward the window.

"So much for the plan to feed her a few yards away so she wouldn't come back," I said.

"We're not getting a cat," he said.

"You know, she's probably really thirsty... maybe dehydrated," I said.

"Well.... I'll go give her some water, but we're not getting a cat," he said once more with emphasis.

After giving her a bowl of water, he settled back onto the sofa. Ten minutes later, the gray furry head appeared again in the window. She raised her paw to mime her "meow" for Tom and then she walked down to the window closest to me and repeated the same pitiful scene. She continued working on us every 20 minutes or so for the rest of the night. The next morning, she was waiting on the deck and rubbed up against the kids' legs when they came out to give her food.

"We're not getting a cat," Tom said, in case I'd forgotten overnight.

"And we're not leaving that cat here to starve, either," I said, which is something he knew for certain I'd say.

We asked neighbors if anyone knew her, but everyone agreed she was a stray, probably dropped off by someone who didn't want her. A neighbor let me borrow a travel crate to put her in, and we packed up our bags and our stray and headed home.

"We're not getting a cat," Tom said during the drive. "This is just temporary until we find her a good home."

Once we got home, I went to the store to fetch a litter box, cat food and a little red cat collar with a bell. We wiped the cat down with some damp cloths to clean her up, and she ate until she was full and promptly fell asleep on the rug, purring her gratitude while the corners of her mouth turned up ever so slightly. The kids circled around her, agreeing she was the coolest cat ever.

"I think we've been adopted by a cat," I said, gently breaking the news to Tom.

"Well, I'm not cleaning that litter box," he said.

"Deal," I said. "I'll teach the kids how to help."

Later that night, I found our new skinny cat on Tom's lap, curled up contentedly while he scratched her head. And I think they've forged an unlikely bond. Tom has worked in sales for his entire career, and this weekend he came face to furry face with a cat who knows one of the most effective strategies for getting what you want: "Ask for the sale." And this cat asked – over and over and over again. She stayed in front of us, and we couldn't ignore her need.

The only thing left to do was name the newest member of the family. So we did. We call her "Percy," which is short for "Persistence."

"One Fish, Two Fish, Three Fish, Dead Fish"

A few years ago, Tom made a mistake. Without thinking through the consequences, he did something rash and now we're both paying the price.

Our oldest son, Adam, was 6 at the time, and he asked his dad for a pet fish.

"You're not really old enough yet to have a fish. You can have a fish when you're 8," Tom said, assuming the fish wish was just another whim that would soon be forgotten.

But some six-year-olds have long memories. A week or so before Adam's eighth birthday, he said "Remember when Dad said I could have a fish when I'm 8 years old? I'm going to be 8 soon!" So what's a mom to do? The deal was done.

It's not that I hate fish. In fact, I enjoy them quite a bit when they're filleted, fried crispy and served with a side of hot hushpuppies. But pet fish are another thing entirely. Yes, they're pretty and soothing to watch, and I like the way the fish tank hums peacefully at night. But fish require maintenance – regular feedings and tank cleaning sessions.

Sure, dogs and cats require maintenance, too, but fish can't repay your efforts by curling up on your lap or wagging their tails when you come home.

There was no going back on the promise, however, so we bought a fish tank and wrapped it for Adam's eighth birthday. He was thrilled when he opened it and could hardly wait to go to the store to pick out his pet fish. His brother and sister went along, too, and when they came home we were the proud owners of three fish – one fish per kid.

Once the fish tank was furnished with brightly colored gravel and a fake pirate ship, Tom released the three small fish into their new home. Their names are Fishy, Floppy and Ralph.

Floppy and Ralph seemed right at home from the minute they hit the water. But I was worried about Fishy, although I didn't mention anything to 6-year-old Jack, his master. Fishy seemed lethargic. He didn't eat much, and he wouldn't join in the fish games with his roommates. We supervised Adam when he fed the fish to make sure he didn't overdo it, and we followed the tank set-up instructions to the letter.

But four days later, Jack came to me right before bedtime and said "Mom, something is wrong with Fishy! Come look!" Of course, I knew exactly what I'd see when we entered the room. Poor Fishy was lying on his side next to the pirate ship, eyes wide open and not a single fin was flinching. He was gone.

"What's wrong with him? Is he sleeping? Or is he... dead?" Jack asked, his voice breaking on that last word while the tears welled up in his eyes.

I couldn't bear it. I rushed him out of the room and into his bed. "Let Dad take a look at Fishy, and we'll figure out what's wrong with him, okay?"

I gave Jack a few books to look at while Tom and I whispered to each other in the hallway. Briefly, I considered sending Tom to Wal-Mart on an emergency fish-run to buy a twin to the dearly-departed Fishy. I was pretty sure Jack wouldn't be able to tell the difference. But then we agreed that, if fish were going to be a part of the household, the kids would have to learn that sometimes fish pass on to the great aquarium in the sky.

So we broke the sad news to Jack, and he cried and I cried with him – not as much over missing Fishy but because a mama can't keep grief from touching her kids' lives. He cried himself to sleep that night.

The next day we told Jack he could pick out a new fish and give him a name. "But I like the name of my first fish," he objected. So we settled on a compromise, and soon Ralph and Floppy welcomed their new roommate named "Fishy 2," a small Tetra with a neon blue stripe. So far, he's proving to be a much healthier sequel to the original Fishy.

Ralph, who belongs to Adam, is a pale red fish who looks like he's on steroids. He's so fat that I'm certain he's eating the majority of the fish food. If he keeps this up, he'll probably be able to bench press the pirate ship soon. And Floppy is a bright yellow fish who is happy to chase Ralph around the tank all day long.

Part of me wishes Tom had never made that promise two years ago, as I know they'll be more fish funerals to come over the years and tears to go with them. But the other part of me knows it's good when kids learn to love another living thing and care for it, even if, at some point, they also have to learn to say goodbye.

153

WE ARE FAMILY

Tom and I kept our end of a deal we made two years ago with Adam. When he was 8 and the last of his pet fish died off, he asked if he could have a dog and we told him that, when he was 10 years old, we'd consider it.

In what seemed like the blink of an eye, two years zipped by. Adam turned 10 and reminded us about the dog promise. I thought of a zillion good reasons why we did NOT need a new puppy right now, -- the house training, the chewing, obedience training, vet appointments, and plenty of extra time and effort.

But I also couldn't deny how much I loved my own dog when I was Adam's age. I want that experience for him, too.

So we began the search for a dog, and – like so many modern match-making efforts – we cruised the Internet to find him. Last week Adam pointed to a small photo on a website and said "I think I found him."

He was a 5-month-old rescued stray being fostered in a town two hours away. His online profile said he was on his way to a Petsmart store where he would spend one Saturday afternoon making sad puppy eyes

at all the shoppers in hopes of being adopted. So we loaded into the minivan and set off to meet him in real life.

During the ride to the pet store, I told the kids this was just a doggie date – not necessarily a dog we'd take home with us. We'd need to make sure he had the right temperament, that he was healthy, that he wouldn't get too big to have in the house. They nodded in agreement.

Then we walked through the pet store doors and caught a glimpse of him – a small, sweet Beagle mix puppy curled up on the lap of a shelter volunteer. I reached out to touch his velvety ear as he looked up at me. And even though he has outgrown the tiny puppy stage, I could tell he was still very much a baby. More importantly, he was a baby who needed a mama. My heart had already taken him in. All that was left to do was the paperwork.

An hour later, we left with a new dog crate, a harness, a leash, some dog food and a new member of the family – Charlie, the Beagle baby. The kids are crazy about him, and so is Tom. Percy the cat is irritated by the whole situation and glares her disapproval. Our 14-year-old backyard dog, E.J., is mildly amused by Charlie's enthusiasm and seems happy to have canine company.

As for me? I can't stop mothering him. He is my "transitional dog." The first time I held him, I found myself swaying back and forth the same way I did when the kids were babies and woke up at 2 a.m. needing comfort.

So far, Charlie is doing really well except for one annoying habit. Often I take him out and exercise all my maternal patience as he leisurely sniffs every tree, bush and blade of grass in our yard. After I'm sure he has had plenty of time to take care of business, we go back inside where he immediately attempts to use my living room carpet as his puppy toilet. Obviously, we've got a lot more training to do.

But that's okay. When sweet Charlie curls up in my lap and has a puppy dream, paws and nose twitching in his sleep, I forgive him for all the extra floor scrubbing. Because he's ours now. He is family.

THE SISSY VERSUS THE SNAKE

The snake sighting in our yard had been haunting me. Every time I stepped outside, I scanned for signs of it – the way wary beach goers check the water for signs of a shark fin.

Then two weeks ago I was home alone with the dogs. Our beagle Charlie got restless so we headed out to the backyard for his potty break. As we hit the bottom of the steps, Charlie ran off to the left and I went right. That's when I saw it – and froze. Another two steps forward and I would have been right on top of a 3-foot-long snake.

The beast was black with red and yellow stripes. As I sprinted for safety, my mind flashed back to that rhyme about how "red and yellow kill a fellow". I scooped Charlie up and flew up the stairs and into the back door, shrieking the whole way.

Instantly I knew there was an even bigger problem than the 5-foot snake sprawled out in the flower bed. If he slithered away, I'd never, ever go into the backyard again. I couldn't call Tom because he's always conveniently away on business when threatening wildlife comes calling. So I called my dad, who would surely rescue me.

When Mom answered her cell phone, I yelled "SNAKE!" And she said, "What? What are you talking about?" (FYI: When a hysterical woman yells the word "snake," it always means she has seen one and needs help right this instant. It's not a conversation starter. It's the same as yelling "Fire!" But I digress.)

I told her about the 7-foot long snake. She said they were at a restaurant eating lunch but would come as soon as they could.

Eating lunch? While your daughter is in mortal peril from an 8-foot snake? I urged them to finish and race to my house as fast as their Buick would bring them.

I waited by the window forcing myself to stare at the 9-foot snake so I'd know exactly where he was when Dad showed up to kill him. When he slithered into the grass, I was afraid we'd lose him. But the snake seemed to know I was watching. He made a large loop and headed back onto the stone patio directly beneath the window where I stood frozen in fear. He was taunting me, torturing me with his slow, menacing slither.

He lifted his head and flicked his forked tongue out over and over again. As he crawled, so did my skin. The hair on my arms stood on end as goose bumps spread over me. Everything in me wanted to look away. But I couldn't. I wouldn't because then he'd get away. When he was just a few feet from the window, I felt it – a tongue on my bare ankle. I screamed and jumped straight into the air, certain the 12-foot snake had slithered into the house to kill me.

But then I realized the wet tongue belonged to the dog, who'd wandered over to see what all the fuss was about. When I shrieked, Charlie yelped and ran to hide behind the sofa. I wanted to go with him.

After what felt like eternity, Mom and Dad showed up. Mom stood beside me and we watched as Dad grabbed a shovel and met the beast on the patio. He delivered a death blow to the snake's head and then flung him over the back fence into the woods, which I'm sure was tough because by then he was at least 15 feet long.

I'm lucky to be alive.

CHAPTER 7

THE JUST-FOR-FUN FILE

Swimsuit Commandments: What Moses Never Told You

"Lo, the time had come and we hastened to the mall to seek out the most worthy swimsuit, for summer was upon us. We sought refuge in the dressing rooms where we squirmed into stretchy fabrics and tied spaghetti straps around our necks. We tugged and hooked and tied and then turned slowly toward the great reflecting glass. And lo, there was much weeping and gnashing of teeth."

And so it was then, and so it is now. The annual hunt for a flattering swimsuit has plagued women through the ages. On the top 10 list of loathsome things to do, shopping for a swimsuit ranks a strong second, right behind the annual gynecological exam.

But no woman should have to go through this alone. Swimsuit shopping is meant to be a team sport. You must seek out your very closest friend, the one to whom you can comfortably bare your cellulite. This friend is your gofer – she gets the bigger sizes while you agonize in the dressing room.

Trust me, you will need someone to agree that the "mirrors in here must be distorting everything." You will need someone to confirm that the "lighting in here is terrible." And, after leaving behind a knee-high pile of rejects in the dressing room, you will need someone to say, "The selection here isn't that great anyway."

Recently I had to face the inevitable hunt. With an honest-but-kind friend in tow, I waded through racks and racks of one-pieces, two-pieces and pieces of pieces that weren't big enough to qualify as cocktail napkins much less swimsuits. I plucked all the "maybes" off the vine and hauled them to the dressing room with a fervent prayer that maybe, just maybe, one of them would look really good.

I tried the first suit on, and I thought it looked okay – not perfect, but it might work – until I saw the rear view. "Next swimsuit, please." The process continued this way until all the "maybes" were piled in the corner of the dressing room floor in a heap of "Hell No!" I wandered back out onto the sales floor in despair, weaving in and out through racks of suits, longing to find just one more "maybe."

I wanted to find the salesgirl, too, so I could grip her by the shoulders, shake her furiously and demand to know where she was keeping the good swimsuits. Had she bought them all for herself? Was she keeping the flattering suits under the counter for all her high school friends to buy? Was there a secret room of swimsuits behind a hidden door, where I could go and find the flattering suits, where the mirrors reflect back an image of Heidi Klum's backside?

After a thorough search of three stores, I found it – the suit that confidently said "yes" when I put it on, instead of screaming "The horror! The horror!" The proverbial needle in the swimsuit haystack had been found.

Tired but grateful, I rushed it to the counter to pay before any other swimsuit warrior – eager to end her own misery – could snatch it from me.

And lo, upon returning home, I repented of the excess fat grams I sinfully indulged in through the long winter. I vowed to keep the swimsuit commandments henceforth, so I might be smiled upon by the lifeguards:

"Thou shalt not smear sour cream on thy burrito."

"Thou shalt not neglect thy treadmill."

"Thou shalt love thy aerobics instructor as thyself."

"Thou shalt not bear false witness about thy swimsuit size."

"Thou shalt sucketh in and hangeth ten."

Amen.

LOVE BRANDS

Tom did something shocking the other day. He came home from the store with a few things I'd asked him to pick up before the snowstorm hit. As I unloaded the shopping bags, I stopped short. I picked up one of the packages, turned it around in my hands in disbelief and then held it up to Tom, as if he'd accidentally brought home toxic waste.

"What is THIS?" I asked.

"It's toilet paper," he said, as if I'd somehow mistaken it for a Crock-Pot.

"I know it's toilet paper, but it's not OUR toilet paper. Since when do we get this kind of toilet paper?" I asked.

"Listen, the store was crowded and this brand was on the end of the aisle and it was on sale, so I just grabbed it," he explained, as if any willy-nilly explanation could be good enough for switching toilet paper brands. "I'm sure it's fine," he added.

He walked out of the room while I glared a hole in the back of his head. You can't go switching toilet paper brands on a person with no advance notice. Some things are just too personal.

By the next day, there was nearly half a foot of snow in the driveway so I had to make peace with Tom's brand selection. I did not like it, mind you, but I tried my best not to complain since we were stuck with it for the time being. Three days later, the snow began to melt and so did Tom's theory about impulsive brand substitutions. As we stood in the bathroom brushing our teeth, he said "You know, I don't like that toilet paper. Next time we go to the store, let's go back to our old brand."

I smiled and nodded, but on the inside I was thinking "Yes, and next time let's not grab the wrong brand just because it's within arm's reach. Some things are worth looking for." (When you're married for a long time, you learn which things are best said internally.)

What those three days with the wrong toilet paper taught me is that most of us are a lot more brand dependent than we like to admit. Sure, we may buy generics on a few things and pat ourselves on the back for saving money, but, for the most part, we love our brands. We grow up with them. And sometimes brands become our buddies.

I read an article recently about a study on brand attachment that was done last year at the USC Marshall School of Business. The results showed that people can be so attached to brands that we suffer separation anxiety when our favorite brands are replaced. (Snippy comments made to husbands are also a common side effect.)

Brand attachments explain why some people panic at the thought of being away from their iPhone for too long. It explains why Pepsi people scoff at the thought of having a Coke. It explains why some teenagers would consider selling a kidney just to have the "right" pair of jeans.

But I, for one, am not ashamed of my brand attachments. I know what I like and I stick to it. Give me a quality product, and I'm as loyal as a Labrador, consistent as a clock. So I offer this poetic vow of consumer devotion to what, for many of us, have become our "love brands".

"I, average consumer, do take you, preferred brand, to be my constant shopping cart companion. You are the Apple® of my eye, and my Gain® is a generic brand's loss. The purity of my commitment is like a Dove® taking flight at Dawn®, soaring across the Quilted Northern® plains. Despite the great Bounty® of brand variety, I will not Bounce® from one name to another, for I am Glad® to forsake all knock-offs and imitations. While others get swept away by the Tide® of change, I enjoy the gentle Febreze® of familiarity. I hold steadfast to my favorites and Nestle® my beloved brands safely into my shopping bags. Truly, I love you All®."

Ode to a Summer Sandwich

We got the first batch of them last weekend, and they were – perfection. Red, round and luscious. Lined up in a shallow, plastic crate, they'd been placed on a sheet of old newspaper, and my mouth watered at the sight of them.

"Oh! Where did you get them?" I asked my parents, who'd just arrived for a weekend visit.

They told me the answer, but honestly I wasn't listening. My mind was racing ahead to the other supplies we'd need: mayonnaise, bread and bacon. After a long fall, winter and spring, my salty beloved has finally returned to me – the bacon and tomato sandwich.

Technically speaking, I could have a bacon and tomato sandwich almost any time of year. They sell the ingredients year-round. But those pinkish imposters at the grocery store can't hold a candle to the honest-to-goodness garden tomato. They are a mere shadow of the real thing. Those robust, red garden tomatoes burst onto the scene around the first of July, like fireworks on the Fourth and every bit as exciting.

My mother fried the bacon extra crispy while I prepared the bread slices by slathering them with mayonnaise. We each arrange our tomato slices and bacon on the bread because sandwich construction is a personal thing. I place the elements with great care so each bite will have its share of bacon and tomato.

With paper plate in hand, I rush my first sandwich of the summer over to the kitchen table and settle in. A tall glass of my mother's syrupy sweet tea sits at the ready on my right. Napkin in lap? Check. This juicy sucker is going to drip all over the place, and I'm ready.

Open. Bite. Crunch. Sigh…Heaven.

I'm lost in the reverie of this most perfect of all sandwiches. In the moment, I don't care about the calories, the salt, the mayo. I don't even care about the artery-hardening evils of bacon. I love bacon. As the bite falls apart in my mouth, I'm not entirely convinced that this isn't worth dying for anyway.

Starting July 1st and running throughout tomato season, I cannot be reasoned with. I'm a bacon and tomato junkie waiting for her next fix. I find myself thinking about them when I should be working or sleeping or paying attention to traffic lights. I crave the crunch, the salt, the acidic twang of a tomato that's perfectly ripe. I shamelessly dream of a bacon and tomato binge. If loving bacon and tomato sandwiches is wrong, I don't wanna be right. The last few bites of my first sandwich of the summer begin to disintegrate in my hands, as the mayo and the juice from the tomatoes soak through the soft bread.

I wash down that last bite with a huge gulp of sweet tea, and my eyes roll back in my head a little as I lean back and relive that perfect last bite.

"There's enough bacon left for a second sandwich," my mother says. "Want another one?"

My eyes widen and I'm fully alert again, reaching for the loaf of bread.

"Do you even need to ask?"

The summer is too short, people. Pass the tomatoes.

LETTER TO MY MACHINES

Dear appliances,

We've been together a long time now. And you're great. Really, you are. I want you to know how much I appreciate all the work you do around here. I don't know how I'd run the household without you.

But the truth is, I need a break. I need an appliance vacation. I'm tired of stuffing clothes into the washing machine every single day. I resent being at the beck and call of the dryer's alarm. I can't just drop everything and rush upstairs to empty it every time it beeps insistently. I've got work to do, kids to feed and another riveting round of Junior Monopoly to play. By the time I get back to the dryer, the load of dry laundry has developed a few thousand wrinkles and is begging for a visit from its cousin, the iron. But I broke up with him years ago. He's still collecting dust at the top of the closet.

So I make peace with the wrinkles and begin the tedious task of folding the clothes. And I fold, and I fold, and I fold. As I run around the house depositing those stacks of folded clothes and towels back into their designated drawers and shelves, I have the strangest feeling of deja vu. Didn't I just fold and put away this very same Elmo t-shirt a few days ago? Then I realize that, yes, I did. After a quick trip to the backyard to play, it landed right back in the washing machine.

Sure, I could take a day off from laundry now and then. Maybe I could even take off a whole week. But we all know I'd end up staring at a mountainous pile of dirty t-shirts, jeans and Spiderman underwear, and it would take the better part of the following week just to conquer that mountain. No, it's not worth it. A load a day keeps the piles away.

Don't even get me started on the dishwasher. He's a huge help but he needs to be emptied nearly every day. I'm beginning to measure my week by how many times I've sorted the forks, knives and spoons. By the time I've reached five or so, I know the weekend must be getting close.

Oh, and the refrigerator. Did you know she's been secretly hoarding dinner leftovers for weeks now? Just today I opened her up and discovered a box containing two-week-old taco pizza that had nearly fossilized. Then I found a forgotten fruit that had oozed juice everywhere. If the oven can clean itself, why can't the fridge have a self-cleaning crisper drawer? How was I supposed to know four weeks had flown by since I cleaned it out? I was busy folding clothes.

I know this letter must make me sound like an ungrateful wretch. I know that, without all of you, I'd be scrubbing that Elmo t-shirt against a washboard and hanging it out to dry. And milk would spoil after only a day. Believe me when I say it's not you, it's me. I just need some space. Even the best of friends need a little time away.

So please understand if I let the lid slam down on the washing machine now and then. Don't hold it against me if I let crumbs pile up in the bottom of the toaster. It's just that there are so many of you who need attention and only one of me. A girl has to get out now and then for some fresh air and sunshine, perhaps a relaxing trip to the mall or hair salon.

When I come back, I promise I'll be better. I'll empty the dishwasher with gratitude and fold that wrinkled laundry. Because we're all in this thing together. Running a household is a big job, and we can't afford for any one of us to break down. Keep the faith, my friends.

Sincerely,
Your benevolent master

The Curse of the Very Safe Place

There's an unspoken law of motherhood: Moms have to know where things are. Men and children believe ovaries also function as homing devices, able to locate anything within a 100-mile radius.

When the kid's backpack is missing, Mom can find it. Husband can't find the mate to his black trouser sock? Mom will uncover it. Need a spare button, a double-A battery, pizza coupon? Mom knows exactly which corner of the junk drawer has all three. Moms are finders.

So it's particularly upsetting to a mother when something is lost and she's the one who did the losing. It happened to me two months ago, just before we began a kitchen remodeling project.

Before work could begin, everything from the kitchen cabinets had to be moved to another room. I moved it all myself, and when the kitchen makeover was finished, I moved it all back again.

I thought everything was present and accounted for until the day the grandfather clock stopped ticking. I went looking for the skeleton key and clock-winding tool – which I've always kept together in a kitchen cabinet – but they weren't there. Both have been missing for weeks now, and I've looked in every logical and illogical place they might be.

173

I distinctly remember moving them from that kitchen cabinet and putting them in a "very safe place" - a place so safe that my little boys wouldn't find it. A place safe enough to prevent the key from getting thrown away in the midst of remodeling chaos. It was so safe that I congratulated myself on finding such a clever hiding spot. But I can't seem to be that clever again. I've outsmarted myself, which makes me a very clever idiot.

Perhaps it's not all my fault. I bet it's partly genetic. My own mom used to sign my report cards and then tuck them away in a "very safe place" so we'd be sure to take them with us to school the next day. Then the next day would come and she'd have absolutely no idea which spot she had designated as the very safe place. I'd roll my eyes at her, certain this annoying habit was something that only happens to old people.

But here I am, certifiably old in my thirties. I've searched and cleaned and searched again, wracking what's left of my feeble mind, desperate to remember where I put the key and clock-winder. "How many very safe places could there be in one house?" I wonder, as I look behind photo frames and inside vases. I've got to find it. I must! Because if I don't, it's going to be 2 o'clock forever on the grandfather clock and, every time I pass by it, I'll be reminded of how terribly smart I was and haunted by the curse of the "very safe place".

Maybe this is God's way of teaching me to accept life's little mysteries or to be patient until a mystery unravels itself when the time is right. Speaking of time, it's still 2 o'clock in my living room and the clock hasn't chimed in months. The silence is deafening. But what can a mother do besides accept her own limitations and hope that, one day, the universe will hand her the answers she searches for.

In the meantime, if you find some report cards, a key and a clock-winder, they're mine.

SMART WOMEN, FOOLISH DESSERTS

Dear Cheesecake,

It seems like forever since we last touched. I know what I said last month, that it was over between us. But I only said it out of fear that this obsession of ours would cause my favorite jeans never to fit again. That was just my own insecurity talking. You knew I couldn't just walk away.

Last week I saw you across a crowded restaurant, teasing me from the silver dessert tray. I would recognize your fine angular shape anywhere. But I was counting fat grams, and I knew one bite would cause me to fall into despair over my lack of self-control.

But a woman has needs. I know that now. Just last night I lay dreaming of you, overcome by a craving so strong I feared I might go mad should I deny you even one more day. So I convinced my husband to take me back to that little bistro where you and I first met. He never suspected for a moment that I was motivated by pure lust.

He's a good man. He doesn't deserve this. But I just can't keep this charade up anymore. "To hell with the light menu," I said. "Tonight I'm having appetizers and dessert!"

He looked shocked, but the wild look in my eye told him it was best to smile and stay out of the way.

After dinner, I asked the waiter to bring you to the table, but he said you weren't on the dessert tray – probably out flirting with other women, I imagine, in some dark little corner booth across town. So I had your brother, Turtle, instead.

I know you're shocked, but please don't be angry. I saw his rich chocolate and creamy caramel and, well, one thing led to another. I was weak.

I wanted you to hear it from me because I think that blabbermouth carrot cake saw us from the next table. She sees everything.

Please believe me when I say it meant nothing to me. He just happened to be there when I was lonely and upset at the thought of losing you to some early bird diner. You know nothing could ever replace you, with your supple, smooth skin – the way it glistens by the light of a single candle. Your creamy texture, your sweet taste.

Even a nibble and I'm wild with desire. I love the way you look dressed up in that deep red strawberry drizzle you wear so well, the way it falls down your sides and pools all around you.

I know you're hurt by my abandonment and betrayal. I know your lightly tanned graham cracker exterior will be tough to break, but I must try. I can't let this thing between us go. Call it obsession. Call it reckless passion. Call it whatever you want.

I call it "delicious."

Eternally yours,
Gwen

CONFESSIONS OF A PRODUCT JUNKIE

Early one morning as I was brushing my teeth, I heard clattering coming from the shower followed by my husband's not-so-chipper morning voice. "Honey! Why are there so many bottles in the shower? I'm tripping all over them. Who needs this many bottles of shampoo and stuff?"

Silly question. Silly man. I replied with a non-answer that usually ends this type of discussion: "It's a girl thing, honey. Just push them aside."

I heard an aggravated groan followed by shampoo bottles falling over and that was the end of that.

I don't expect him to understand. His entire grooming regime consists of two things – soap and shampoo. On a trip, he can fit both into a sandwich bag, and he can't imagine why anyone would need more than that.

But there are countless women – and you know who you are – who suffer from the same costly addiction I do. We're product junkies. We've never met a moisturizer, lip gloss or facial cleanser we didn't want to try. At least once.

Shopping for beauty products is like dating. A woman can't just scan the shelves and instantly know which product is the one for her. No, she has to take it down, handle the bottle, smell it, buy it, take it home and try it.

In a perfect world, that product would be just right for her. She and the product would have a long, happy life together and she would never look at another product again. But alas, it's not a perfect world. Sometimes the eye cream we had such high hopes for just doesn't live up to our expectations. We begin to wonder if there might be something better out there. Something to diminish fine lines the way we've always dreamed of.

Before we know it, during what's supposed to be a quick trip to Wal-Mart for milk and bread, we're drawn back to the health and beauty aisle, scanning the shelves for a product to fall in love with. Sometimes we have to go through this trial and error process several times before we find a handful of products that live up to their marketing claims and make us feel like a natural woman.

Because we have a complex grooming ritual, women go through this selection process for several types of beauty products – everything from shampoo to foot cream. We don't need just one shampoo. Sometimes we need a hydrating shampoo. Sometimes we need an extra deep conditioner. Sometimes we need a clarifying shampoo when the deep conditioner has left us with "product build-up". Sometimes we need body wash with exfoliating beads. Sometimes we just want the creamy stuff that smells like peach mango.

Sometimes, when we have extra time, we need leg shaving gel and foot scrub. And sometimes, when we're pressed for time, we need the two-in-one shampoo plus conditioner.

Most ladies play the field until they find the ideal products. Some of us – the hard core product junkies – do research. I pick up a few women's magazines and scan the table of contents. When I spot an article titled "Beauty editors reveal their top product picks," I can't flip to that page fast enough. I tear out the page, stick it in my purse and I'm ready for the next trip down the health and beauty aisle.

But what happens to the products that just don't work out? We can't throw them out because they're not empty. We can't give them to a friend because it would be obvious the products had received a mark of disapproval. And we certainly can't let them take up valuable bathroom counter space. So they eventually migrate to the far reaches of the cabinet under the sink – where beauty products go to die. They languish in this product purgatory until the day we run out of storage space, and then they finally meet their fate at the bottom of a trash bag.

We know it doesn't make any sense to the men in our lives. It's not supposed to. There are plenty of things we don't understand about them. In the meantime, when he trips over shampoo bottles or discovers the product graveyard under the sink, just toss your deeply conditioned hair to the side, smile and say, "It's a girl thing, honey."

CHAPTER 8

THE HOLIDAY FILE

HOT TAMALES ON VALENTINE'S DAY

Not long ago, in the week leading up to Valentine's Day, my husband casually accused me of being unromantic. "That's absurd," I thought. "Of course I'm romantic. I'm a woman, aren't I? Romance is biologically tied to ovaries and estrogen, so I'm sure I have plenty of it. It's an inborn trait."

I brushed off the comment as trivial, but, in the back of my mind – where a woman stores all her husband's seemingly casual comments – the statement stuck. Then it got me wondering: Have I changed?

My gut knew the answer before my head was willing to admit it. I have changed. Life has changed. And it has changed me. My only consolation is knowing I'm not alone. So this is for all of us who know, deep down where the truth hangs out, that somewhere along the way we went from being a fiery hot tamale to a mild, lukewarm taco.

There was a time early in our relationships when we were likely to strew rose petals from the front door to a bubble-filled bathtub encircled by candles. There was a time when we left behind little love notes, when we called just to say "I miss you." We treated ourselves to nightgowns that made a big impression.

Fast forward several years and a few kids later. The only trail from the front door to the tub consists of Lego blocks and Goldfish crackers. Those little love notes morphed into sticky notes on his mirror that say "Remember to pick up your dry cleaning." These days, many of us can't help but glance at the price tag on a silk nightgown and automatically think to ourselves that the same amount of money would buy two pairs of kids' sneakers at Shoe Carnival.

For me, I think subtle changes began as soon as he lifted the veil and the minister pronounced us husband and wife. That word, "wife," it carried a weight. A girlfriend can be fun, flirty, even wild. But a wife? A wife should be proper. I struggled to reconcile who I was with my new role and what I thought I "should" be.

As soon as I figured out how to be a respected wife without being June Cleaver, that little home pregnancy test turned positive. I wasn't just somebody's wife anymore. I was a mother. Motherhood is such a big, overwhelming concept that it sometimes swallows up everything and everyone in its path – including the flirty girlfriend you used to be. I think I lost my groove thang somewhere between the epidural and potty training.

Motherhood has a way of turning even the most spontaneous, carefree woman into a practical mothering machine. We have such a long list of things that need our attention: immunizations, the food pyramid, potty training, stain removal, toddler hygiene, stranger danger, house cleaning, birthday parties, and on and on. So flirting, unsolicited compliments and spontaneous backrubs either get shoved way down the list or fall off completely.

It's not because we don't like those things. It's just that they seem like the least urgent items. They also seem a little selfish – a word most of us think no "good mother" should ever be associated with. We forget that what often seems like a selfish time-out for a backrub is really self-preservation. It's essential to protecting the relationship that started all this mommy stuff to begin with.

All that being said, I'm still a realist. And reality dictates that there will be times when all I want is to put on my husband's baggy t-shirt, skip shaving my legs, collapse into bed and sleep alongside the man who promised to love me in good times and in hairy-legged exhaustion.

Parenting is a big job, and some days it drains you. I don't beat myself up for those days when my romance meter registers a negative 24. It happens, for moms and for dads.

The good news is that even the most tired tacos are not typically short on love or affection. It's there. It's just suffocating under layers of responsibilities, worries, time-demands, and a whole lot of laundry. But love and affection can and will flourish when they meet up with a little time and attention. For most women, it's the time and attention that are so hard to come by. That's why trusted babysitters are so critical to the health of a marriage. It's why "dating your spouse," as corny as it sounds, is a big deal.

Sometimes all you really need is a few hours away, on a regular basis, to remember that underneath all the wife stuff, underneath all the mommy stuff, you are still you. An interesting, fun-loving, spicy you.

THE MOTHER'S DAY QUEST

Something happened to me about four years ago that I never wrote about. Even though it was huge, I never said a word, which is odd when you consider how writers typically use almost anything, including mundane trips to the grocery store, as writing material.

But something tells me Mother's Day is the right time to finally tell it. So here goes:

Tom and I had been married about a year and had just moved back to my home state where he took a promotion and I got a dream job of my own. We bought a house, settled in. Things were on track, and we felt ready to have a baby. So we waited for that positive pregnancy test. And we waited. And waited.

After seven months of waiting, I went to the doctor to complain about the waiting. He ran some tests and discovered that my body ovulated on a random, infrequent schedule so he put me on medication designed to increase our odds of conception.

The medication worked and a month later, we finally saw that positive pregnancy test on the bathroom counter. About 10 weeks into the pregnancy, we went to the doctor's office with a blank videotape.

They'd told us to bring one so we could have a copy of the baby's first ultrasound. But as the doctor scanned my abdomen, the screen was blank. Just like that, the baby was gone.

I'll never forget that overwhelming feeling of disbelief as the doctor said – in a tone that was so terribly matter-of-fact – "Well, there's no heartbeat. That happens sometimes. We'll schedule surgery to remove it. Would five o'clock today work for you?"

When I didn't respond, he must have sensed the avalanche of emotion about to crash down on me. So he left the room quickly and let his nurse pick up the pieces. I spent the rest of the day in a fog. After the surgery, I was grateful for how sleepy I was because I didn't want to be awake. When I was awake, I felt hollow, hopeless.

You wouldn't think 10 weeks of pregnancy would be long enough to fall in love with someone smaller than a green pea. But it was and I did. I fell in love the second that test stick turned positive.

Like so many women who've been through a miscarriage, I reeled from the shock. It felt as though we'd been cruising through life in a convertible with the top down on a sunny day and then suddenly we slammed head-on into a brick wall. No warning. We went from happy to devastated with one awful phrase – "no heartbeat."

I did what most women in this situation do. I got up every day, cried in the shower and went to work to try to get on with things. A few weeks after it happened, Tom and I went to dinner with friends who knew about the loss. The emotional pain was still so fresh for me. We sat through dinner and no one said a word about what had happened. By the end of the night, I felt even worse. There was a dead baby in the room and no one would even acknowledge it.

In hindsight, I know our friends weren't being insensitive. Like so many people, they just didn't know what to say or if they should even try. So we all just pretended there was no lost baby and no broken hearts.

Eventually, I was approached by friends and relatives who'd also gone through miscarriages I'd never known about. When it happens to you, you join a silent sisterhood of women who share a sorrowful bond. They all encouraged me to try again, and I knew I would.

There are so many women – including those who have endured miscarriage after painful miscarriage or years of frustrating fertility treatments – who are still trying. It begs the obvious question: Why? Why risk the emotional devastation over and over again if the odds aren't in your favor?

And the answer is this: You do it for the slim chance that you might get to be part of a miracle. And the miracle is worth it. It's worth it.

Whether through fertility medication, in vitro or adoption, becoming someone's mother is a miracle. What wouldn't you do for a chance like that?

Fortunately for me and Tom, my next pregnancy, although difficult, culminated in the birth of our son, Adam. Two and a half years later, we were blessed with Jack. But I'm always mindful of how lucky we are. Because things aren't automatic. Our bodies don't always cooperate with the desires of our hearts.

On Mother's Day, there are millions of women on a quest for motherhood. Despite month after month of disappointment, they persevere. They keep trying and waiting for their own miracle. Mother's Day is not just for women who've done time in a delivery room. It's also for the adoptive mother who scooped up a child who needed her. It's for the mother who loves foster children. And it's for those special women who are "like a mother" to a child who desperately needs one.

Motherhood is a state of being. It's a loving heart. It's looking past yourself to cherish someone else's happiness. It's compassion, tenderness and strength. So many women on the quest for motherhood are already "mothers" in the truest sense of the word. They're mothers waiting for a child to come along and soak up all that love.

My prayer for you is that child will indeed come – in whatever way God intends it – and will bask in your love and reflect it back to you in the amazing way children do.

Keep trying. Keep striving to find a way to the child your heart dreams of. I can only imagine how hard the journey is. But I'm certain it's worth it.

Godspeed.

THE BUTTERFLY MOMENT

Though I'm giddy about the new life bumping around in my very pregnant belly as well as my amazing two-and-a-half-year-old son, Adam, I know that Mother's Day is not all flowers and Hallmark cards. For many people, it's bittersweet and sometimes even painful.

Every year there are children who are missing their mothers on Mother's Day. And there are mothers desperately missing and mourning children. My own mother is one of them.

On every other significant day of the year – my brother's birthday, Christmas Day and even the anniversary of his death at age 34 – she somehow manages to get through the day pretty well. Though the pain of his loss is undoubtedly with her on those days, she keeps herself busy and focuses on all the wonderful memories she has of him. Everybody, including me, is amazed at her strength.

But Mother's Day is different. On Mother's Day, the pain bubbles up through this permanent crack in her heart, and it would be impossible for her to hide how much she misses him. She always appreciates the flowers, cards and gifts we give her, but all she really wants on Mother's

Day is to be with me and my brother, Greg. So his absence is especially sharp on the second Sunday of May.

But leave it to God to use special days like this to remind us that even death doesn't sever the mother-child bond. Last year, something happened on Mother's Day that still makes the little hairs on the back of my neck stand up.

Before I tell this story, you should first know that, shortly after my brother died, his memory took on a kind of symbol – a yellow butterfly. It all started when his gravesite was literally swarmed by them one day. Ironically, in dream interpretation, butterflies symbolize someone who has undergone a transformation and is now in a happier place.

In the three years since his death, all of us who loved him have had our share of "butterfly moments" that seem to come along when we need them most – just simple reminders of Greg and what he meant to us.

But the most remarkable butterfly moment happened to Mom last year on Mother's Day. After an emotional morning, Mom and I took the Jeep Cherokee my brother used to drive to a discount store so we could pick up some lawn chairs she wanted for the front porch. I was driving and she was in the passenger's seat. After we parked, we started trying to fold the backseat down so we could fit the bulky chairs in the back.

After a few minutes of fiddling with seat levers and getting nowhere, I looked up to the sky and said jokingly "Okay, Greg. We might need some help here." All we were hoping for was a little heavenly assistance with the seats, but we got a lot more. About two seconds later, I heard Mom gasp and say, "Gwen, you're not going to believe this. Look!"

I looked and there, on the floorboard under the passenger side seat, was a yellow butterfly. It was not alive, but it seemed to be because its wings were spread out perfectly and it was not crushed or damaged in any way. It was as if it had been perfectly preserved just for this moment.

Mother's Day
May 11, 2003
Love, Greg

I knew instantly this was no accident, no random butterfly sighting. It was my brother's clever way of giving Mom a gift she could hold on to – proof that his spirit was very present. "Mom," I said. "It looks like you just got your Mother's Day gift from Greg." And for the first time that day, there was real joy on her face because she knew it was true. He had sent the butterfly just for her.

Perhaps it had been lying there for months waiting to be discovered. Or perhaps some invisible hand had placed it there just a moment before Mom folded that seat back and found it. It's impossible to know for sure.

We carefully scooped it up and put it in an envelope to carry it home. She had it mounted in a small shadow box along with an engraved tag that reads "Happy Mother's Day 2003, love Greg."

And if her house ever catches fire, God forbid, I know that butterfly in the shadowbox will be the first and perhaps only thing she carries out of there. Because it is precious beyond all other things. It represents physical proof that the love between a mother and her child is truly forever.

THE FIREWORKS STAND

We waited impatiently for the first day of fireworks sales and the glorious moment when those wooden flaps would be propped open on the yellow stand with the exploding red firecracker painted on the front.

When it finally happened, summer came alive. My brother and I were always in the first wave of kids to line up at the stand, desperate to get to the front and peer into that concession stand full of loud pops and brightly colored sparks. We bought our favorites – Roman candles, bottle rockets, parachutes, jumping jacks, smoke bombs, sparkling fountains and Texas chasers. We bought anything that looked and sounded new, anything we hadn't tried the year before.

We didn't just dabble in fireworks; we stocked up, as if that fireworks stand might never open its wooden flaps again. We bought bottle rockets by the gross – 144 explosions in a pack. We bought enough Black Cat super-loud firecrackers to make every one of our neighbors nearly deaf from continual blasts. We spent our entire summer allowance and then some, anxious to compare notes with the other kids in the neighborhood in the traditional show-and-tell of "What did you get?"

Our mother dreaded the day the fireworks stand re-opened nearly as much as we counted on it. Her idea of safely enjoying the Fourth of July was having a mature adult – wearing a welder's hood and rubber gloves – light one firework at a time while the children and their mother watched from roughly four blocks away. Sure, you couldn't really see or hear the fireworks from that distance, but at least everybody was safe and no one lost fingers or got an eye put out.

My older brother had different ideas – like lighting an entire packet of bottle rockets at one time. He held the end of a smoldering punk stick in his mouth while he carefully threaded the fuses of the firecrackers together. Once everything was ready, he lowered the punk stick to the frazzled end of the fuse and waited for a spark to catch and sizzle up the line. He quickly backed away a few paces and braced for the "RAT-TAT-TAT-TAT," as the staccato shots pealed through the streets.

But that was before I grew up – when the Fourth of July was about food and fireworks and fun by the pool. Now that I'm older, I realize that the Fourth is also about what freedom costs, about the high price of independence. Some families have paid that price in the most personal way. Those are the ones who really know how precious freedom is.

I think about them when the fireworks stands open each year, the day the sparklers are lit, the day we carve turkey, the day we deck the halls, and every day between and every day after. We are blessed to live in a free land we call "home."

VAMPIRE'S BLOOD

It was an unusually warm October afternoon, and my brother Greg and his pack of neighborhood buddies were up to no good. Greg was about 12 years old and I was 6 that year. He loved Halloween, nearly as much as Christmas. He looked forward to it, planned for it.

Greg and his friends had this little clubhouse behind our home. It wasn't actually a house but rather an overgrown box hedge that lined the alley behind the backyard. The boys had tunneled into the tall, thick hedge and carved out a small meeting space where they'd huddle together and talk about – well, I have no idea what they talked about because the hedge was strictly off-limits to little sisters. But on that day, I – the youngest little sister on the whole block – was invited into the boys' super-secret wooded cave, a high honor indeed.

I crept through the scratchy branches until I came to the clearing where the boys were sitting around a flashlight and a box of Halloween supplies including fake eyeballs, Pop Rocks candy and green face paint. My brother pulled out a tube of "Vampire Blood", which was a thick, red gooey liquid that looked alarmingly real. He said he had an idea for a great joke. As he smeared the red gore on my forehead, temple and into my blonde hairline, he gave me these instructions:

"Here's what you do. After we put this Vampire Blood on your head, you'll run into the house and scream really loud like something is wrong or you're hurt or something. Mom will think it's really funny when she finds out it's just fake Vampire Blood."

"She'll think it's funny? Are you sure?" I asked.

"Yeah, don't you think it's funny? C'mon. We'll be outside waiting for you," he said.

"Yeah, it's funny! I can do it," I said, eager to please and entertain.

With fresh fake blood dripping from my head, I prepared for my starring role in what was supposed to be the very funny Halloween joke of 1979. The boys watched through the sliding glass door as I screamed my bloody head off and sprinted through the back door and into the kitchen where Mom was washing dishes. She spun around, saw my head and grabbed me by the shoulders. "What happened? What happened to you?" she said frantically.

But my brother had failed to give me any lines to say during the "joke," so I had no idea what to tell her. With no backstory, I just kept on screaming for dramatic effect. Nobody anticipated what happened next. She picked me up, turned me sideways and stuck my head under the kitchen faucet. She frantically ran her fingers through my wet hair, searching for the source of all that bleeding.

The Vampire Blood washed away leaving behind nothing but the evidence of a prank gone wrong. By the time she realized I wasn't dying of a traumatic head wound, I was drenched, flustered and mystified as to why my brother hadn't come in to explain that this was supposed to be the really funny part.

Mom wasn't laughing, and the mastermind and his cronies had wisely fled back to the safety of the clubhouse hedge. The next several minutes were filled with angry finger pointing and loud lecturing about how I should never scare my mother half to death. I tried explaining that the boys had said it would be funny, but – having just had a year shaved off her life by pure fright – she was in no mood for excuses. My brother hid out until things cooled off. As for me, I learned valuable lessons that day:

1) Plans hatched inside a box hedge are probably not on the up-and-up.

2) Vampire Blood is water soluble and won't cover up a lie.

3) Mamas never think bloody head wounds are funny – ever.

What's Wrong with This Picture?

Six-year-old Jack and his dad have a Sunday morning tradition. They like to flip to the back page of the comics in the Sunday paper and try to find the six differences between two similar pictures in the Slylock Fox cartoon strip. It's sort of a race to see who can find all six differences first.

Brain teasers like this one have been around for a long time because they tap into something people do almost automatically – notice what's wrong with the picture. I don't know if it's human instinct or something we're taught as we grow up, but we're all pretty good at it. Give us a field full of daisies and we'll notice the one dead flower in the middle of all that glorious yellow. Our eyes are drawn to the flaw, that thing that's just a little bit off, no matter how insignificant it is.

We do it in our lives, too. We look at a career full of wins and think mostly about the screw-ups or the missed opportunities. We look at a healthy body that works perfectly fine, and we notice how our belly isn't as flat as we want it to be. In our homes, we see the floors that need new carpet or the kitchen that needs new appliances and miss out on seeing everything that's right – like strong walls, a solid roof, warm rooms, hot showers, and a fridge full of food – basics that so many people around the world just don't have and probably never will.

As people who've been blessed with so much, Thanksgiving is exactly the "kick in the butt" holiday we need, forcing us to take off the "what's wrong" goggles that magnify every imperfection and, instead, marvel at all the things that are so wonderfully right. And there are a lot of them.

Granted, it's easy to forget about the good stuff sometimes. Our 24-hours-a-day news culture has a bad habit of finding the horrible, the weird and the controversial and serving up a piping hot dish of it during every hour of the day and night. Good news is harder to come by but it's equally as important.

When we strip life down to what matters most to us, it's so much easier to see what's right with the picture – family, food, safety, health, freedom, love. It's great to strive for things to be better or to reach for the ideal, but never noticing how good we have it would just mean we're being jerks. And ungrateful jerks are the very worst kind.

So here's to all that's right with the picture. Here's to the carpet stains that remind us what a luxury it is to have carpet and food and drinks to stain it with. Here's to the belly that's no longer as firm as it once was and to the babies it allowed to grow inside us. Here's to the thousand little "wrongs" that only prove how "right" we've got it.

FLAMING ANGELS AND
AILING WISE MEN

'Twas the week before Christmas when I got a splinter in my eye that nearly ruined everything. I was 7 years old and all set to be Wise Man No. 1 in the annual church Christmas play the next day.

What first felt like a pesky eyelash soon began to feel like a fence post jabbing at my eye. I rubbed, blinked, cried. Nothing worked. That night, it woke me from a deep sleep.

The morning before the show, my mother took me to the doctor who ordered me to lie down on a table. Then he turned my eyelid inside out for a better look.

His eyes widened and he quickly said, "My God... Nurse, come look at this." I panicked. I felt like a science experiment gone wrong. My mother was sure I was either going blind or dying or both.

The "foreign object" (fancy doctor-term for splinter), had left an impressive number of eye scratches, so the doctor covered half my face with a huge eye patch. I thought the patch was pretty cool until I remembered my approaching stage debut. How could I go on as Wise Man No. 1 looking like I'd just survived a bad camel crash?

The doctor said it was fine to go on with the show, telling my mother I might be a little clumsy while adjusting to the patch.

There weren't enough kids in the church to find a replacement, so my mother said we'd tell people a desert storm blew sand in my eye on the way to see Baby Jesus. That evening, I put on my robes and headed for church.

With the candlelight service set to begin, I lined up right behind the Angels on High and prepared for the procession down the church aisle toward our cardboard stable. Some of the older kids playing Mary and Joseph had already taken their places by the manger in front of the pulpit.

The pianist started playing "Silent Night" which was our cue to start down the aisle carrying lit candles. It was all going well until I smelled smoke.

In my haste to get down the aisle, I got my candle a little too close to the lacy wings of Angel No. 3 right in front of me. My depth perception was off because of the patch.

A church deacon spotted the trouble as we passed his pew and he quickly grabbed the angel and started beating her smoldering wings. Angel No. 3 didn't realize her wings had been ignited, so the beating felt more like an assault. The procession of angels and wise men came to a thudding halt.

After Angel No. 3 was thoroughly checked out by her mother, our Sunday school teacher decided we should begin the procession again in a desperate attempt to save the remainder of the play.

Angel No. 3, with her charred wings, was promoted to the front of the line so she wouldn't have to stand near me, the half-blind Wise Man who nearly torched her the first time. And my mother blew my candle out before I started down the aisle again, just to be on the safe side.

The second procession attempt went perfectly, and we made it to the manger just fine. The narrator was wrapping up when my friend, Wise Man No. 2, started to look pale and shaky. She'd always been the kind of kid who got sick when she was nervous, and I guess the flaming angel incident combined with stage fright took its toll on her stomach.

She dropped her myrrh, covered her mouth for a moment and then brushed me aside as she attempted to leave the stage. She made it as far as the manger and then threw up all over everything, including the Rub-A-Dub doll that was being used as Baby Jesus.

Mary and Joseph turned as white as the fake sheep, and the narrator quickly ended the play by saying, "We hope you've enjoyed our play." The audience didn't know whether to clap, laugh or call emergency medical personnel.

It's been more than 20 years since that Christmas play, and it's still one of the most memorable in church history – the half-blind wise man, the flaming angel and the wise man who tossed her cookies in the manger.

There will never be another Christmas play quite like it.

'Twas the Day After Christmas

'Twas the day after Christmas and all through the house
Not a creature was resting, not even a mouse.

Crumpled paper and boxes were heaped by the door
In hopes that the trash men might take a little more.

The children were running and jumping with glee.
It was the day after Christmas. They had new toys, you see.

And Mom in her sweatshirt she bought at the Gap
Knew it was highly unlikely the children would nap.

When in the guest bathroom there arose such a clatter,
We sprang from our sofa to see what was the matter.

Away to the noise we flew like a flash.
Had someone fallen, did a finger get smashed?

When what to our sleep-deprived eyes should appear
But a wide-eyed toddler shedding real big tears.

He had stood by the toilet and then in a rush
He pitched in small toys and gave a quick flush.

He panicked and hollered, so quickly we came,
And he stood there and cried while he called them by name:

203

"Oh Hot Wheels! Oh Sponge Bob! Oh Care Bear! Oh Doggie!"
None of them could swim and were all getting soggy.

From the tiny red racecar to the square yellow doll,
They swirled away, swirled away, swirled away all!

Though it might cost more than a brand new Hummer,
We had no choice but to call in a plumber.

As we consoled our toddler and were turning around,
Down the driveway the plumber came with a bound.

He was dressed all in denim from his head to his feet.
It was beginning to snow and he was covered in sleet.

A bundle of tools he had flung on his back,
And he looked like a peddler just opening his pack.

His eyes how they twinkled! His smile how merry!
From the patch on his shirt, I knew his name must be Larry.

He said not a word but went straight to his work.
He extracted the toys and then turned with a jerk.

We apologized for the work but he said it was fine.
After all it was Sunday, he'd be paid overtime.

He said he loved kids and bent over Baby Jack
And despite what you've heard, there was no plumber's crack.

A wink of his eye and a twist of his head
He gave me my invoice and there was nothing to dread.

He climbed in his pick-up and started it up
He backed down the driveway with his red coffee cup.

But I heard him exclaim as he drove through the mush
Happy New Year to all and don't let that kid flush!

Gwen Rockwood lives in Northwest Arkansas with her husband, Tom; their three kids, Adam, Jack and Kate; two dogs, Earless Joe and Charlie; and one adopted stray cat, Percy. Her parents, Wanda and Billy Rule, live right around the corner. When she's not folding laundry, she writes an award-winning weekly column called The Rockwood Files, appearing in newspapers in Arkansas, Missouri and Oklahoma and in *The Village Family Magazine* in Fargo, N.D. Her work has also appeared in four editions of the *Chicken Soup for the Soul* book series. Visit her online at www.therockwoodfiles.com and at www.nwaMotherlode.com.

Photographer Lisa McSpadden lives in Northwest Arkansas with her husband, Glen, and their two active and adorable boys, Josiah and Caleb. They're excited about the upcoming arrival of their third child. She specializes in newborn, child, maternity and family photography. Her fun sessions put children and families at ease and capture each child's spirit and true expression. See more of Lisa's work at www.LisaMacPhotography.com and on Facebook at www.facebook.com/LisaMacPhoto.

CPSIA information can be obtained at www.ICGtesting.com
Printed in the USA
BVOW03s1850110215

387388BV00001B/89/P